The Sunsphere
In
Knoxville, Tennessee

written by

Martha Rose Woodward

Dedication:
This book is dedicated to my pal, Doug Young (1949-2013).

ISBN-9 781499 258066

The Sunsphere as seen in 2011 by World's Fair historian Bill Cotter of Los Angeles, California. (Photo used by permission of Bill Cotter/Aug. 25, 2011).

People say

 People say it looks like a giant microphone rising up from the sidewalk. People say it should be open to the public so that the citizens can enjoy the panoramic view from its top. People say it has magical powers and should be worshipped.

 On the other hand, people say it is a useless building which cost too much and continues to absorb tax dollars which could be better spent somewhere else in the city's budget. People say it is cursed and that nothing good will ever come to it because of the Butcher Banking Scandal which left numerous citizens of Knox County in financial peril. People say it should be torn down and the steel and glass should be sold as scrap.

 People say a lot of things about the Sunsphere, however, it continues to stand, tall and serene, like a soldier, guarding a city.

 Whatever people say about the unique tower that was built as a monument to the sun, the story of the Sunsphere is a story that needs to be told. This book is, basically, a biography, or the life's history of a landmark, from its beginning as a thought in the mind of a visionary and continuing through over 32 years.

 The Sunsphere is a complex, 266 feet steel and glass tower which has stood tall and straight for over 32 years with its golden windows glistening in the sun as a monument to the sun, and it all began with a thought.

Author's Note:

Method to the Madness

In order to help the reader to get the perspective of the story of the life of the Sunsphere, I have organized the manuscript into a time line spanning from 1971 to 2011. I chose 1971 because that was the date in which Kyle Testerman was elected as mayor of Knoxville. It was some time during the four years of his first administration, 1972-1976, when the suggestion of a World's Fair began to take root. Steward Evans is given credit for having the idea in 1974. It was the making of the World's Fair that gave us the Sunsphere.

Some of the years on this timeline are basically empty. As one Park Patrol officer said, "Not much has gone on in the Sunsphere for several years." That in itself became part of the story. Some years were busy, while others were pivotal in this story.

Also, I have kept the information for each year as it is an island until itself. I want the students and scholars who may use this book in order to learn about the history of this landmark to be able to turn to any date and be able to see what happened during that year. This causes me to repeat some of the information. I made the decision that it would be a more accurate record of history if I presented the same information from various sources.

Kindest regards,
Martha Rose Woodward

The Thought

In 1974, the mayor of Knoxville was Kyle Testerman. Mayor Testerman and other city leaders were searching for something to do in Knoxville which would revitalize the downtown area and encourage development of 72 acres that were seen as an eye sore. Not much was there except trash, empty boxes, bit and pieces of old cars, and wood and bricks from former buildings. The land was used mostly by rats and the homeless. With the news that the World's Fair in Spokane, Washington had helped to revitalize the parts the city of Spokane which were suffering from neighborhood blight, the mayor began asking civic leaders to develop a plan. The idea of holding a World's Fair in Knoxville was hatched because Spokane, Washington and Knoxville, Tennessee were seen as truly similar cities. Both had about the same population, both needed renewal of their downtown areas, and both were located near larger metropolitan regions with natural beauty around, as well.

Mayor Testerman assembled a 17 member bipartisan committee and appointed Jake Butcher, a local banker, as the president of that group. A feasibility study of all past World's Fairs was ordered so that Knoxville could begin to get some ideas of how the city could benefit from investing in redevelopment, which having a World's Fair could bring. From the recollections of most people involved in the decision making processes in those days, it was Stewart Evans, president of the Downtown Businessman's Association, who pushed for a World's Fair to be held in Knoxville. Although Mr. Evans has passed away, he lived a long and productive life.

In 1975, a handsome, young Democrat named Randy Tyree defeated the Republican, Kyle Testerman. The results of the election were seen as quite a feat, since Knoxville has been a stronghold for Republicans since the War Between the States. Testerman had begun to make enemies with all the talk of a World's Fair, and he had a problem with garbage workers and, at one point, fired 300 people. Many of the citizens of Knoxville were also against the thought of raising taxes in order to pay for what was being called "their fair." "Their" was referring to the advisory board.

When Randy Tyree, at age 34, took office in 1976, the plans for a World's Fair were on his desk. Mayor Tyree saw the idea of a world's fair as an urban renewal project. Mr. Tyree was 100% in favor of the exposition picking right up where Mayor Testerman had left off. He appointed a committee known as KIEE or Knoxville's International Energy Exposition to work on the fair, naming Bo Roberts as the president of the committee, and Jake Butcher its chairman.

When the Democrats won the presidential office in 1976, Tyree and Butcher worked with their many friends in the party, including President Jimmy Carter, and Carter's Budget Manager, Burt Lance. President Carter came on board for the idea of a World's Fair in Knoxville after meetings with Jake Butcher and Mayor Tyree.

Jake Butcher had a history with Burt Lance having done business with him for several years. It was

Jake's bank that had loaned money to Burt Lance when Lance was a businessman in Georgia. This gave Jake Butcher access to the President of the United States. The persuasive banker convinced President Carter to help Knoxville with grant money from various agencies in the federal government. President Carter came through for his fellow Democrats who had, after all, helped him to get elected as president.

President Carter helped the city of Knoxville to get permission from the Bureau of Internationle Fairs (BIE) in Paris, France. The letter President Carter wrote proclaiming the permission to hold the fair was printed in the local newspapers in 1978.

1978   President Jimmy Carter

A city doesn't just up and have a world's fair. It must get permission from several agencies first. That sort of permission generally involves help from the Office of the President of the United States. Working with President Jimmy Carter, Mayor Randy Tyree, Jake Butcher, and Jesse Barr were able to get the permission they needed. On December 6 of 1978, President Jimmy Carter wrote the following proclamation announcing that the world was coming to the city of Knoxville.

Proclamation 4628—Knoxville International Energy Exposition of 1982
December 6, 1978

In May 1982, a six-month International Energy Exposition will open in Knoxville, Tennessee, inviting the nations of the world to think anew of man's relationship with the pervasive force of energy which fundamentally shapes the choices people have as to the endurance and enjoyment of life itself. This exposition, whose theme is "Energy Turns the World," will provide a splendid setting in which to explore new technologies to conserve energy, to harness the long-lasting and most renewable sources, and to carry on the search for new sources of energy.

Because of the opportunities which the Exposition offers for a deeper understanding of energy issues and for the stimulation of trade and cultural exchange, this Administration is moving to extend the fullest possible recognition to this event in accordance with Public Law 91-269. On April 26,1977, I advised the Secretaries of State and Commerce that the Exposition warrants Federal recognition as provided by statute. On April 27,1977, upon request of the United States, the Bureau of International Expositions officially registered the event as a Special Category exposition by unanimous vote.

Also, in accordance with law, I shall appoint a United States Commissioner General to exercise the responsibility of the United States Government for fulfillment of the Convention of November 22, 1928, relating to International Expositions, as modified, and to invite the several States to participate.

Now, THEREFORE, I, Jimmy Carter, President of the United States of America, in further recognition of the International Energy Exposition, do hereby authorize and direct the Secretary of State to invite, on my behalf, foreign countries as he may consider appropriate to participate in this event.

In WITNESS WHEREOF, I have hereunto set my hand this sixth day of December, in the year of our Lord, nineteen hundred and seventy-eight, and of the Independence of the United States of America the two hundred anniversary.

Signed by JIMMY CARTER

1977-1982 Creationism

The Knoxville International Energy Exposition Board met every Friday at noon to discuss ideas and plans. One of the leaders who was involved in the planning was Litton Cochran. Cochran visited the offices of a local architectural firm, Community Tectonics, which was created by Hubert Bebb, in November 1979. William Denton was the chief architect for Community Tectonics at that time, and was present for the visit from Cochran.

Cochran had stopped by Community Tectonics on other business concerning the restaurants they were working on for him. After he and the firm were done with their discussions about the restaurants, Cochran suggested that the Fair needed a theme structure. This suggestion put William Denton into the thinking mode. He knew that the theme of the fair was energy, and he began to think about the fact that all energy comes from the sun. He decided the theme structure should be something about the sun, and it was decided that a "monument to the sun" be built. Needing to be able to make a presentation to the management committee for the Fair the next morning, Cochran asked Mr. Bebb, and Mr. Denton to develop not only some ideas, but, a written plan, as well.

It was at that time, an afternoon in November, 1979 that Hubert Bebb began to doodle and sketch, while William Denton and Don Shell worked on a written presentation. Don Shell was a young architect, at that time, who had recently been hired by William Denton.

Mr. Bebb drew three sketches, and William Denton came up with the name Sunsphere. The staff at Community Tectonics worked into the night creating the ideas for the theme structure, and delivered the presentation to Mr. Cochran's mail box in time for him to take it to the scheduled meeting. The original sketches which Bebb made on that day are kept in the files of Community Tectonics on Coward Road in West Knoxville.

Mr. Bebb's idea was for a huge golden globe to be supported by a tower. William Denton quickly came up with all sorts of ideas which involved facts about the sun. Mr. Bebb's first ideas presented the globe as hovering on the ground or only being supported by a short tower. Formerly, he had designed the tower at Clingman's Dome in the Great Smoky Mountains National Park. Clingman's Dome contains a ramp that winds around the tower and allows hikers to walk steadily up the mountain while winding around the center of the structure. Mr. Denton liked the idea of a ramp winding around the dome and this was used in the first model made of the Sunsphere. There would be four models made of the new theme structure before the design was tweaked into the shape that we have come to recognize as the golden 74 foot globe sitting on a 192 foot tower.

"We knew that we wanted the sphere," said William Denton, "that part of the concept never changed, although we did go through changes to the size of the sphere, and to the interior décor."

The KIEE Board immediately liked and approved of the plans, however, as the management committee of the Fair worked with the concept, there was more discussions about making the tower tall enough to be seen from all parts of the 72 acres where the Fair was going to be built. Knowing that the Space Needle in Seattle, Washington rises to over 600 feet, the KIEE Board pushed for the Sunsphere to be that tall. Construction cost and time prevented this from happening. The total height was finally set at 266 feet.

The site of the Sunsphere was chosen because that was the only place left in the park that had not been claimed by some other building. Community Tectonics ordered testing of the soil. This brought bad news. The site contained approximately 33 feet of clay. This meant they had to do more digging. The building was eventually set in over 20 tons of concrete, in order to give it the stability needed for a tower of that height.

According to William Denton, the Sunsphere actually stays erect by the same principal as a floor lamp. The base is heavier than the top. If the force of the wind is up to 100 mph, the strength of the concrete in the base is stronger than the tower, therefore, if the tower is acted upon by a force, such as a wind, it might tilt or sway, but, it will remain upright.

Taking the ideas from the sketch pad and turning the plans into a 266 ft. steel and glass structure would be a long and difficult task. People who were directly involved on the construction of the building remember the entire event as a nightmare while others saw it as challenging. The word that came up the most often in their memories was codes. "Codes, codes ,codes," said one man. "They nearly shut us down with plumbing, electrical, fire, city, county, state, and federal codes." (interviews)

Jake Butcher--President of Knoxville's International Energy Exposition

Not only did President Jimmy Carter get the Knoxville International Energy Exposition Board to give permission to hold the fair, he also came through with help in arranging for money to fund the fair to the tune of millions of dollars. There were four main sources of money appropriated through President Carter to be used for the Worlds' Fair. These sources were:

$5 million from an Urban Development Action Grant. The $5 was supposed to be used to incorporate a hotel on the premises which could be used well after the fair.

$4.25 million from the Economic Development Administration for land acquisition, demolition and preparations.$1.5 million from the Appalachian Regional Commission; $500,000 was the allotment for the state of Tennessee from ARC, which made the total $2 million.

$600,000 from the Secretary of the Interior's discretionary fund for land and water conservation. This grant was supposed to be matched by local and state funds, bringing the total to $1.2 million.

This money was a great start, more would be needed, and more was on the way in the form of grants that would help Knoxville to do something about its roads and highway system, which, at this time in 1978 would not support the traffic to be caused by a projected eleven million visitors.

Former President Jimmy Carter and his wife, Rosalyn visited the Butchers and the World's Fair on October 9, 1982. While gazing out the mirrored window of Jake's United American Bank, the Former President said, "obviously one of the best decisions I made while I was in office was to help Jake Butcher with the World's Fair." Less than one month later, federal regulators were sent to audit the banks which were included in the Butcher Banking Empire. That audit would discover that Jake's banks were over $90 million dollars in debt, with only $40 million in capital. Jake Butcher had driven banks that were once in solid financial shape down into bankruptcy. . (Knoxville Journal, 1983)

Former President Jimmy Carter has never made a public comment about the Butcher Banking scandal. It is not known if he continues to believe that his decision to help Jake Butcher was one of his best ones.

1971-2007
Who's Your Daddy?

To put the story of the Sunsphere into perspective requires background information about the people who were mayors of Knoxville during its conception, birth, and up to the present date. This section will repeat some of the information you have already read, but, it is important to include the details again.

In 1971, Kyle Testerman, a Republican, was elected as mayor, and assumed office in 1972, serving a four year term. It was during his administration that idea of hosting an international exposition was hatched. Stewart Evans, the then President of the Downtown Knoxville's Businessman's Association, is given credit with having pushed for the idea of a fair like the one in Spokane, Washington. In 1974, Kyle Testerman appointed a 17 member, bipartisan advisory committee to conduct a feasibility study on the possibilities of having a World's Fair in Knoxville. Mayor Testerman chose Jake Butcher, a dashing, young banker, who was a Democrat, to chair that committee.

In 1975, Randy Tyree, a Democrat, was elected mayor, taking office in 1976, serving for four years. The 34 year old Tyree was the youngest man every elected to office as mayor in Knoxville. He won the election by approximately 350 votes from over 50,000 votes that had been cast. This caused the new mayor to get the nickname "landslide Randy."

The election of 1975 turned out to be a "barn burner" with votes being counted twice in some precincts. When the dust had settled, the city found itself with a new face in the mayor's chair. Many people were stunned, since Mayor Kyle Testerman had been well-managed and well-monied.

It was during 1976 that the Knoxville International Energy Exposition was formed. Many of the same individuals who had been named by former Mayor Kyle Testerman on the exploratory committee were also in KIEE. Bo Roberts was named as KIEE president, with Jake Butcher as chairman. Jesse Barr was their financial advisor and deal maker.

Jake Butcher's bank had once loaned money to Burt Lance, a businessman from Georgia. Burt Lance was close friends with Jimmy Carter, who appointed him as manager of the Office of Budget Management. Because of his relationship with Burt Lance, Jake Butcher was able to get a meeting with President Carter. Jake asked President Carter for help in getting permission for the City of Knoxville to hold a World's Fair. President Carter signed on for the project and sent a formal letter of permission in 1978. President Carter was also instrumental in getting federal grants for the road construction and urban renewal that was desperately needed in Knoxville.

In 1979, when Randy Tyree was one again elected to office, he became the first Democrat to serve for two consecutive terms. He assumed office in 1980, serving until 1984. The city was satisfied with its mayor and returned him to his office so that he could complete the job of managing the exposition.

It was Mayor Tyree who saw the span of the development of the World's Fair. He was along for the ride as it went from an idea all the way into reality. He faced numerous battles along the way, especially from a group of vocal citizens who were against the fair.

It was said that 76% of the citizens in Knoxville were in favor of having a referendum, 50% said they would vote against the fair, and 34% said they were in favor of it. They kept pushing for the mayor and city council to put the issue of the fair onto a ballot and let the people vote for it or against it. There was never a vote. This left most citizens angry and bitter. People were mostly against the heavy burden of the tax increases which were put into place in order to finance the fair. It appeared to the citizen group, Citizens Against the World's Fair, that the city was paying for private businessmen to make money from their investments in the fair. (8-8-79, Knox News-Sentinel)

Randy Tyree ran for governor of the state of Tennessee in 1982, adding fuel to the flames for the vocal group of citizens who saw him as an opportunist. Citizens were thinking that Mayor Tyree needed to spend his time working as mayor, and forget state politics. Mayor Tyree lost the governor's race in 1982 to Lamar Alexander by a 40% to 60% vote. Mayor Tyree did not run for office of mayor in 1983 paving the way for former Mayor Kyle Testerman to recapture the mayor's chair.

Former Mayor Randy Tyree is remembered as an excellent mayor and a truly fine person. He returned to the private sector earning his living by being a lawyer. He and his wife, Mary Pat, raised four wonderful children and continue to be well-liked and admired in the local community. The general population of the city of Knoxville has fond memories of the former mayor who was known for his movie star good looks and his attractive wife. The handsome mayor and his beautiful wife were often lovingly called "Ken and Barbie." They look back on these nicknames with fondness.

In 1983, Kyle Testerman easily won the election and served until 1988. The community turned to the former mayor in hopes that he could clean up the financial mess which had occurred when the Butcher Banking Empire had fallen. Mayor Testerman faced numerous problems during his term after the fair, mostly because of that scandal. There were layers and layers of deals, loans, grants, and unkept promises for him to sort through. The city needed someone in office who had experience, and Mayor Testerman apparently rode back into town with guns a' blazing. He provided a steady, experienced hand at a time when the city needed one.

Many who remember the mayor's second term as successful, also remember two issues which were hurtful to his reputation; (1) a very public divorce, and (2) Mayor Testerman's rejection of the Fairfield Redevelopment Plan which may have provided for a better economic post fair Knoxville.

In 1987, Victor Ashe, a Republican, was elected as mayor. He served his first term until 1991 when he ran again for office and was reelected. Mayor Ashe was elected and served for a total of four terms or sixteen years from 1988 until 2004. In 2004, Mayor Ashe was term-limited out of office.

In 2003, even though the city elections are said to be "non-partisan," Bill Haslam, a Republican, ran for office and won a close election against Madeline Rogero, the Democrat. Mayor Haslam ran for a second term in 2007 and was easily elected against candidate Isa Infante, who ran to keep Haslam from running a non-contested race. Voter turnout was dismal as less than 15,000 voted. Infante received 1,000 votes with Haslam receiving the others. (Wikipedia search, mayors, Knoxville, TN)

Governors in Tennessee Serving From 1974-2011

1974-1979	Ray Blanton
1979-1982	Lamar Alexander
1982 -1987	Lamar Alexander
1987-1992	Ned McWherter
1992 -1995	Ned McWherter
1995-1999	Don Sunquist
1999-2003	Don Sunquist
2003- 2011	Phil Bredesen
2011-	Bill Haslam

In 1973, Lamar Alexander, a Republican, ran against Ray Blanton, a Democrat, for governor of the state of Tennessee and lost. However, in 1977, Ray Blanton did not run for re-election due to turmoil concerning the report that prisoners inside the jails in Tennessee were paying the Governor for pardons. Blanton's troubles paved the way for Jake Butcher to run against Alexander, however, Alexander won the election.

This was a tough blow to the arrogant banker who was accustomed to having everything he wanted. One issue that seemed to have been a turning point in the election occurred when a news anchor of one of the three major television stations reported that Jake Butcher's home, a mansion named Whirlwind, actually had more bathrooms that the Governor's Mansion in Nashville. This news did not sit well with the rural citizenry and may have influenced enough votes to reject the flamboyant millionaire.

After taking office, Alexander was able to put politics aside, as he helped the city of Knoxville with issues surrounding the World's Fair, often working side by side of his former opponents.

In 1981, Mayor Randy Tyree ran against Governor Alexander for the governor's seat, but lost, leaving himself deep in debt and in trouble back at home where citizens were upset with him for taking his political dreams statewide. As governor, Alexander was able to implement the much needed changes to the educational system bringing in a Master Teacher's Plan known as Career Ladder which was a merit pay system which paid the better teachers more money. Throughout his 8 years in the governor's mansion, the popular Republican was often called upon to deal with the aftermath of the Butcher Banking Scandal, making ethics the focal point. Ironically, the ethics of the Butchers had been the issue Lamar Alexander had campaigned on since his first race.

The Butcher Brothers' Scandal turned out to be the fourth largest banking failure in United States history. (Knoxville Journal, 1983, Borrowed Money, Borrowed Time).

November 1979 CommunityTectonics

Hubert Bebb (rhymes with web), created the architectural firm now known as Community Tectonics in 1966. Mr. Bebb, who lived to be 81 years old, was an experienced designer who had worked for other World Fairs as well as in numerous businesses in the East Tennessee area. His chief architect, William Denton, designed the mansion, Whirlwind, for Jake Butcher.

Denton says that the task of taking a dream and turning it into a large monument is almost unimaginable. Numerous hands touch the project, while hundreds of meetings need to be held. Getting permission for the various items needed for the project can be seen as challenging or as being a nightmare. Not only did the architectural firm have to deal with architects, construction workers, plumbers, electricians, carpenters, painters, builders, there were also the political aspects that crept into the deal. Individuals from Knoxville to Nashville, and as far away as Paris, France came together to make the dream a reality. There were times along the way when the people at Community Tectonics and the Board at KIEE thought that the Sunsphere would never be built. However, with perseverance and commitment, and with the purpose of coming together as a community behind the idea for a World's Fair, each person worked tirelessly, day by day, to see the project through to its end.

Don Shell, currently the Chief Executive Officer at Community Tectonics, was a witness to the origin of the Sunsphere, when at age 25 in 1982, he sat across the desk from Hubert Bebb and William Denton as
Mr. Bebb drew the sketches which, eventually, became the Sunsphere.

Shell and William Denton recall the events with, basically, the same highlights. Each adds pieces and segments the other may have forgotten. (interview Don Shell)

Interview with Don Shell, June 4, 2007 Offices of Community Tectonics:

In 1979, the KIEE Board was looking for a theme structure for the World's Fair. Community Tectonics had done some work designing restaurants for Litton Cochran. He mentioned to the Board that Hubert Bebb and William Denton always had good ideas, so, he asked them to generate a written plan which would include drawings. Bill Denton knew that the theme for the fair would be energy, and he began to think about the sun as the source of all energy. His original concept was to put the sphere on top of a small pedestal that would have a ramp up to the top. However, once the concept was set into motion, members of KIEE, especially, Jake Butcher, wanted it to be a tall tower that could be seen from everywhere in the fairgrounds. He also wanted people to be able to go up inside and view the sights, as well as see to the Smoky Mountains. This information was not known to the architects on that day in November when they were making the first plans, however.

Unfortunately, Litton Cochran needed the plans the very next day to present to the KIEE Board. Hubert Bebb, William Denton, and Don Shell worked late into the night on the plans and sketches, and had them ready in time for Mr. Cochran's meeting at eleven a.m. the next day.

Also, the KIEE had no money for a theme structure. They asked Community Tectonics to not only design, and build the Sunsphere, but to find the financing as well. The financial deal was put together, after a lot of work by lawyers and members on the KIEE Board. Jesse Barr was one person who worked to bring the deal together. When the Sunsphere was built, three parties were owners: Community Tectonics were part owners; First National Bank of Louisville, Kentucky put up a $5.2 million loan, The City of Knoxville put up $1 million federal grant, which was supposed to be used on the Sunsphere, repaid, and used again for Urban Renewal. William Denton, Robert Woodson, and Dr. Robert Morris were the men who signed as guarantors, with the City of Knoxville in the second position on the loans.

"We put ourselves on the line in order to make the Sunsphere happen," said William Denton. "Luckily, Dr. Bob Morris and I sold our shares to C.H. Butcher. It is unclear, but, I think Bob Woodson lost most of his investment in the property."

Albert Finley was an attorney who worked with Jesse Barr to close the deal. Investors refused to sign on until they knew details and that the design could actually be built. Bankers could not agree to lend money on the project until they had exact facts and figures detailing costs and who would be doing the work. Construction companies could not commit to doing the building without details, as well. All of these problems fell onto the shoulders of the architects at Community Tectonics, mainly William Denton, who had to face each situation, and come up with answers.

The main problems, as with all public buildings, were the rules and regulations which fell under "building codes". Knoxville did not have any codes in place which dealt with a structure or tower of this sort. Fire safety codes, plumbing codes, electrical codes, elevators, drainage, safety, and more were hurdles which had to be jumped. There were times when the architects thought that the idea of the theme structure would never come to reality.

However, after hundreds of meetings, and after numerous discussions with city officials, the firm received final approval from the City Council and Codes Enforcement. At this point, Community Tectonics, Rechinbach's and others went into a building frenzy.

The Knoxville International Energy Exposition was advertised as a time for all countries of the world to come together to learn about energy. At the groundbreaking ceremony that signaled the beginning of the building of the Sunsphere, the group was given shovels and hard hats and told to smile for the camera. Construction began in January 1981. Architects and engineers continued to face major problems for the thirteen months it took to build the Sunsphere.

"There was a time when we thought we were not going to be able to find glass that could be tinted into a golden hue," said Don Shell. "We had contacted business after business and had been turned away. We thought that we may have to settle for silver windows, however, at, what seemed like the last minute, we found a company in New Jersey that agreed to our specific needs. They made the 360 golden window panes we had envisioned in our plans. Those windows cost $1,000 each; a lot of money in those days."

"When the topped off ceremony was held, everyone's spirits were high," said Don Shell. "We had fought the dragon and won, and we were glad to see the steel in place. We knew we faced more challenges, but, the when the shape took place, the community could see our vision."

A big party was held in April of 1982 with a cake which had "reality" written on the top served to the excited and relieved guests.

*Writer's note: A topped off ceremony is traditional for steel workers. When all the steel is in place for a building, a flag and green tree are placed on top.

1980
Big Dreams
If William Denton, chief architect for the Sunsphere, had had his way, the Sunsphere would be a much different structure than what it turned out to be. Denton wanted to make the structure all about the history of the earth. He planned for art and sound to tell the story of history from Precambrian and Azoic era all the way up to the present Age of mammals, or Cenozoic era. He proposed a 160 foot tower having a diameter of 86.5, which symbolized the 865,000 diameter of the sun. Each floor would have wall murals, paintings, graphics, sound, and color. The first floor would have the rock, dust and gas development of the Precambrian and Azoic Era. The second floor would house the rocks and fossil development of thee Precambrian and Proterozoic era. Floor three would exhibit the age of fish during the Paleozoic era, and also include a restaurant. The fourth floor would be devoted to the age of birds and dinosaurs of the Mesozoic era, with more dining area included. Age of mammals in the Cenozoic era would have been on the fifth floor, with more dining space there, as well.

For some of his other ideas of William Denton was to make a sixth floor which would honor the age of space and a future era. This level would be a cocktail lounge during and after the fair. The two levels which would hold the dining areas would rotate around the sphere, taking one hour, so that while people were dining, they would see the panoramic view. He also wanted to use the colors that were speculated to correlate with the inside of the sun. The sun is said to have a white inner core and a yellow to orange outer core, with dark orange and red as the crust which makes for a gold appearance. He also planned for the Sunsphere to be made of solar bronze glass which would allow it to glow like the sun during the day, and with the use of lights, appear as a sunset at night.

These lofty ideas were the victims of the chopping block as costs grew because of codes enforcement and other considerations. (interview, July, 2007)

Architect William Denton in his office in Morristown, TN in 2007 discussing the Sunsphere with writer, Martha Rose Woodward. Photo by Barrett Buie

1980 KCDC

During the week of November 26,1980, the Knoxville Community Development Corporation (KCDC) approved final plans for the building of the Sunsphere. William Denton and Don Shell , architects for Community Tectonics, presented a scale model of the structure to the group, and explained its design and uses. The estimated cost, at that time, was said to be $3.7. This number changed, almost daily, and eventually included the $5.2 million dollar loan, the $1 million dollar grant, and $400,000 in change orders, bringing the total to $6.6 million dollars. In 1981, and Hardee's Restaurants installed equipment said to be valued at over $1 million, but an exact accounting of the final cost of expenditures by Hardee's is not known. (Womack, R., 11-16-80)

1981 Actual Levels

There is often confusion concerning the levels or floors contained in the Sunsphere. This seems to occur because the three levels on the ground are sometimes counted as one, two and three, while, at other times, the levels in the ball are counted as one, two, three, four, and five. On the original plans the names of the five levels which are in the globe are levels 1 to 5. These levels are actually from 192 to 266 feet in the air.

If the Sunsphere were a typical building, it would have 26 floors, at 10 feet per level for the 266 feet of total height. The tower is 192 feet, the globe is 74 feet.

The levels on the ground are known as levels one, two, and three, while the five levels in the globe are four, five, six, seven, and eight.

Level 1 is the Ground Level. This level of the structure contains three elevators; two are passenger elevators and face the Amphitheater, while one is referred to as the "service" elevator and is at the back of the Sunsphere which faces the new convention center. When the Sunsphere was first built, the elevators had doors which were made of glass. People marveled at the magnificent view as they rode up and down the shaft. The original elevators were replaced in 1991 and were encased in vinyl siding. The vinyl visually distracts from the original design of the steel tower.

Hardee's Fast Food Restaurant was located on Level 1 during the Fair. At the time of the Fair, Hardee's built a separate section to the ground floor which was made of cinder blocks and was attached to the right side of the Sunsphere on the ground floor. During the Fair there were numerous picnic tables topped with colorful umbrellas installed on the sidewalk in front of the Sunsphere facing the Amphitheater. This provided tourists with a place to sit and eat as well as shade from the hot sun. There were also tables at the back of the Sunsphere in the exact spot where the new convention center now sits.

The design of the tower allows for an inner and outer base of steel, which provides strength and spreads the load needed to support the upper 5 floors. From a bird's eye view, looking down on top of the Sunsphere, it is actually hexagonal in shape at its base.

Level 2 contains mechanical and electrical equipment. It is possible to reach this level from the back side of the tower.

Level 3 is the Bridge Level and is flush with Clinch Avenue Bridge. It contains a porch or deck which sprawls out over the sidewalk allowing as many as 150 visitors to gaze at the water and other sites below. During the Fair, the deck became a popular place to sit and rest at picnic tables while watching as the crowds of people mingled throughout the fairgrounds.

There are two sets of stairs which are to be used as a fire exit. Each set of stairs contains 418 steps. The stairs are located in the center of the tower, and are said to be steep. Park Patrol employees report that it is as difficult to climb down the steps as to climb up them.

Level 4 is also known as the Observation Deck, and is the floor onto which most visitors are taken. It has a capacity of 86 people at any one time. Many people think that the view from this floor is the best view from any of the floors because the windows appear to be larger from this vantage point. It is also said that people standing in Level 4 were better able to look out at the park and see what was going on. The architects who built the sphere, however, say that there is not that much difference in the view from level to level. It is possible to see the Smoky Mountains from over 200 feet in the air, and to see the City of Knoxville, the University of Tennessee, the Tennessee River, and all points of interest from any level of the tower.

During the six months that of the World's Fair, large viewers were installed on level 4. By placing a quarter in the viewer, a person could turn the viewer in all directions and see several miles into the distance. Similar viewers are seen throughout the Smoky Mountains and on Lookout Mountain in Chattanooga. After the fair was over, these viewers were sold as scrap, or stolen.

Level 5 is known as the kitchen level and also contained The Blue Room. All food was prepared on this level and moved to other levels by a series of electric "dumb waiters" which look like small elevators. During the 6 months of the World's Fair, the restaurants were busy. The menu included Sunburgers and a drink called Sunburst which was served in glasses which were the shape of the Sunsphere. Heavy Vulcan gas ranges and other equipment which included stoves, huge refrigerators, prep tables, a walk-in cooler, and a walk-in freezer, and more than 20 tables and chairs were placed there. Much of the equipment had to be hoisted into place inside the globe before the glass was installed. This equipment was abandoned by Hardee's Restaurant in 1984, and had fallen into ill repair. It has been reworked, and is in use by Southern Graces

Catering & Events who opened for business September 1, 2007.

When the Knoxville Welcome Center and Visitor's Bureau operated from the site, the restaurant equipment was not used. It is estimated that the cost to dismantle and haul the heavy pieces away would have been astronomical, which would explain why the equipment sat unused for numerous years.

The Blue Room in Level 5 was set aside as private dining space for 38 people. It was called the Blue Room because the walls were covered with blue velveteen fabric while some walls contained mirrors, as well. The Blue Room also had a special lighting system installed which included long, thin rows of lights which made the place sparkle at night. Cloth napkins, silver, china, and reservations were needed in the Blue Room. Meals typically cost from $11.95 to over $20. This was a considerable amount of money for that time period.

I was present for the last day in the life of the Blue Room. My son, Barrett Buie, and I happened to be in the Sunsphere the day the President of Southern Graces Catering & Events Planning, Robert Sukenik, was meeting with contractors and interior decorators who tore into the historic walls and floors in order to update the décor. I was saddened to see the historic decor leave the Sunsphere.

Level 5 is known as the VIP Lounge, and was used by Jake Butcher, his family, and friends as their personal property during the six months of the World's Fair. This level was used by reservation only for other people. It was the place in which all celebrities and those who were kept around to entertain the celebrities were taken. The parties, use of alcohol, and romantic interludes which have occurred on Level 5 of the Sunsphere are legendary. It was a regular occurrence when the Fair had closed for the day, from May until October in 1982, for limousines to pull up to the Ground Level of the Sunsphere, and the wealthy and elite partygoers to be ushered from their expensive cars which included Rolls Royces and Cadillacs, straight up to the VIP Lounge. While there they dined on expensive foods including lamb chops and lobster tails. They drank the best wines, liquors, and beers that were available at the time.

It is quite possible that only the Butchers and their friends knew that Level 5 was being used in this way. I have spoken to numerous people who dined in the Blue Room during regular business hours and who said that they had no ideas about the parties being held after hours.

Levels 6 and 7 were known as The Sunsphere Restaurant. These levels were said to seat 130 to 140 diners. Some plans estimate the total number of diners as being 350 to 376. Guests who dined in the Sunsphere Restaurant were also required to pay the $2 fee to ride the elevator to the top. This was a sore point for some customers who vowed they would not return to the restaurant because of this $2 fee. The typical prices for meals in the Sunsphere Restaurant were from $4.95 to $19.95. This seemed excessive at the time. There was a variety of items on the menu including steak, fish, chicken, salad and sandwiches.

Level 8 is the Mountain Observation Deck and is said to provide a better view of the Smoky Mountains. This may be only the opinions of a few, however, because it is possible to see the mountains from each of levels 4 to 8.

Although the Sunsphere appears to be closed on the top, it is not. It is covered by, what amounts to a large, golden tarp. This removable covering allows for maintenance, as well as access. Inside the ball at the top, there is an eight foot ladder which is attached to the middle of the tower, and a trap door, which can be opened by slinging back the hinge. There is also a large, steel pole which stands above the sphere, and is used when there is a need to attach anything to the top of the steel trusses. This pole also holds lights which blink on and off and are a way of signaling to aircraft that might stray into the path of the building.

I have heard architects refer to the top of Level 8 as being like "standing in the middle of a donut." Picture a circle and how it would be to stand in the center of that circle while being 266 feet in the air--that is what it is like to be at the tip top of the Sunsphere.

There have been times in the history of the Sunsphere when entertainers were buckled onto the steel pole and placed on the tip top of the globe. This looks frightening from the ground, however, once you see what is up there, you can see that if the person is in the center of the circle, he/she is not hanging over the edge of the sphere. If a person were to slip, they would probably only fall about four feet, because the globe is open. There is a circular walkway inside the top of the globe as well. I personally have witnessed Mickey Mouse being up there, and Miss America. There was also a time when a piano player, Jason D. Williams, stood on his head on the top of the globe while playing the piano. He was tethered to a steel pole on ropes. Members of his musical group were up there with him, and it was all truly amazing.

A local basketball hero, Dane Bradshaw, had himself tied onto the top of the Sunsphere, onto a zip line that he rode down onto the grass in front of the Court of Flags for the 25th year's Celebration of the Sunsphere on July 4, 2007. When he got to the ground he told reporters that he was afraid of heights.

There has never been an accident involving any person who has done stunts from the top of the Sunsphere.

There are two small restrooms, one for women, and one for men, on levels four, five, six, seven and eight. Water is pumped up the 192 feet tower with large pumps located in Level 1. Water and sewer pipes flow downward, as well. The restrooms were made handicapped accessible which was done by the staff even though this was not a federal requirements at the time the tower was built. The decision to make the restrooms handicapped accessible was seen as forward-thinking at the time and has saved countless dollars. (Siler, Charles,10-4,1981,Knox News-Sentinel)

Bo Roberts

The name Bo Roberts comes up frequently in research concerning the Sunsphere. Mr. Roberts was president/executive director of the Knoxville International Energy Exposition, and by all accounts, he was an excellent manager and a fine person His contributions to the city of Knoxville are noted and appreciated by everyone who has ever known him. He dealt with all aspects of the World's Fair. In my attempt to make this book more about the Sunsphere and less about the World's Fair, I limited the scope of my research and did not include information from Mr. Roberts. However, he made the following statement which is of public record: "In a short time leading up to the fair, there was a billion dollars' worth of construction on the interstates, the fair site and downtown. The significance of that much money pumping into the local economy can't be underestimated. If nothing else, fair-related spending protected the Knoxville area from the recession that battered the national economy in the early 1980s. We were sort of insulated in East Tennessee from the slowdown that was going on in other parts of the country."

Bo Roberts now lives in Nashville, Tennessee where he is managing partner of NetCom LLC, a strategic planning company. (www.knoxnews.com/kns/local , 7-7-07)

In November 26, 1981, as the Sunsphere was completed, an article was published in the Engineering News Record Magazine which is a monthly journal for professional engineers, and is printed by the McGraw Hill Company. "Energy Expo explores new spheres," and a photo of the Sunsphere was on the front cover.

An article entitled Far Out Designs Add Flair to the Fair gives technical details about the Sunsphere. This is what is said:

Monument to the Sun. The fair's theme structure, called the Sunsphere, was designed as a "monument to the sun," says project architect Bruce B. Thompson *of Community Tectonics, Inc. Knoxville. Interior lighting will make it glow at night through the gold-tinted glass. The 1902 ft. hexagonal steel tower tapers from 110 ft. across at the bottom to 34 ft. across at the top, and the sphere itself is 74 ft. in diameter.

Although it is smaller and shorter than the 118 ft. dia aluminum geodesic sphere atop the 50-story concrete Reunion theme tower in Dallas, the Sunsphere's designers had a very different concept in mind. Reunion's lightweight sphere carries no floor loads, but the surface framing of the Sunsphere is used as an integral part of the structural support for the restaurant and observation decks inside.

General contractor Rentenback Engineering Co., steel erector Jim Everhart Erection Co., Chattanooga, and fabricator Asheville Steel Co., Asheville, N.C., worked closely with the architect and structural engineer Stanley D. Lindsey and Associates, Ltd. Nashville, to develop a design that would keep construction costs within the $4 million budget.

The tower has six double columns, arranged in a hexagonal plan and stiffened with K-bracing. The inner columns of each pair continue up through the sphere, the outer columns stop at its base.

The sphere is framed from 30 vertical curved steel columns and 13 horizontal steel hoops, all 5x3-inch tubes. Structural engineers Socrates A. Ioannides and Jack H. Horner say tubing was selected because it is esthetically pleasing and carries axial loads efficiently. At each of the five interior floor levels, beams radiate from the core to the curved columns. The columns support the weight of the skin, wind loads, and parts of the loads from the interior. The horizontal hoops share in these loads as well as serving to stabilize the columns. Loads from the 30 curved columns transfer back to the six core columns through a tension ring at the top and a compression ring at the bottom, both of which are essentially space frames constructed from tubes ranging from 14x14 inch by 6x6 inch. Tubes were used in all these areas because of their good torsional capabilities.

Although the fair site is located over an area of cavernous limestone, and most buildings in the area are founded on caissons or piles to solid rock, engineers determined that the stability of the Sunsphere would allow use of the spread footings and grade beams over engineered fill instead of a costly deep foundation, a savings of $80,000 to $100,000. Above the fill, the core columns rest on a combination mat footing. Grade beams extend from the mat to the footings of the flaired external columns which rest on individual spread footings. The flaired columns footings are connected with grade beams, forming a hexagon on the perimeter.

* The name Bruce B. Thompson was wrong.

Jesse Barr 1982

Making It Happen; the Go-to Guy

In writing this historical account of the Sunsphere, I soon realized that the one person I needed to talk to the most was Jesse Barr. Although other people had the ideas, drew up the plans, and did the actual building of the monument, everyone will tell you that the man who put the financial deal together to make the Sunsphere happen was Jesse Barr.

Jesse Barr is often spoken of as "Jake's right hand man," a title which he does not shy away from. He continues to beam with pride at even the mere suggestion of that title.

"I was there from the beginning," he stated to me, during our first phone conversation on June 1, 2007. I had found Jesse Barr at the Dean Stallings Ford Dealership where, at age 70, he continues to work. My friend, Lillian Bean, former Knox County Court Clerk, suggested that I call Jesse, and she knew just how to reach him. He was friendly and eager to talk. We spent about fifteen minutes on the phone that first day, and quickly set up a time for a longer conversation. I asked his permission to record that meeting, and he readily agreed to allow it.

Jesse Barr is a Southern gentleman. He is the kind of guy you can be with for about two minutes and feel like you have known him forever. He is full of knowledge, and has a quick wit. He recognizes the mistakes that he made in his past, yet, he has moved on. As a former history teacher, he also recognizes the historical perspective of any story about the Sunsphere, and he was on board for my idea immediately. At age 70, he continued to have plans for the future. He is a deal maker and a friend to many.

"This is great!" he said. "I am glad to hear that you are doing this. The time is right. I will help you all that I can."

Jesse Barr was raised in Mississippi, working his way through school and serving in the Army. He completed a Masters' Degree from Rutgers, and lived in Memphis, Tennessee where he got a job in a bank. He worked his way up through the ranks, becoming a loan officer and, finally, executive vice-president of Union Planters Bank.

In 1976 Jesse was convicted of 25 counts of bank fraud and was sent to jail for those charges, including fraud and receiving kick-backs for making loans. He served his time in jail and was let out early for good behavior. Sometime during the 1970's he was introduced to Jake Butcher and the two became fast friends. Jesse moved to Knoxville after he got out of jail and went to work for Jake.

Jesse had the reputation of a man who could "turn a can't into a can". He continues to be the kind of person who makes you feel like you can accomplish your goals. It certainly speaks to his abilities of charm and charisma when it is shown that a convicted felon went from being in jail in 1976 to being in charge of multi-million dollar deals by 1980 with businessmen practically standing in line to get his attention. People who know Jesse Barr will tell you if you want something done, Jesse is the guy to go to.

Although Jesse and Jake made a lot of things happen around Knoxville, they steered from the legal path out into the realm of the illegal, taking the banks, and many people down with them. Jesse was sent to jail for the second time in his life and it nearly killed him. When the house of Butcher began to fall, Jesse was like the children's rhyme, "All the king's horses and all the king's men couldn't put him together again."

"When the loans came due in 1983, why did none of the owners step forward to pay the payments?" I asked.

"The revenues produced by the Sunsphere during the six months of the fair were placed into a big pot, so to speak. The money was not separated and held in different amounts in order to pay for the loans. It was used daily to pay bills. After things went down the way they did, and Jake's banks collapsed, no one wanted to throw good money after bad," explained Jesse.

"Why didn't the Sunsphere produce enough revenue to pay for itself?" I asked.

"The Sunsphere made money during the fair, however, once the fair was over, the crowds were gone, and there was no way to get enough people up and down those elevators to bring in enough to pay the loans," he said.*

"What did it cost to build it?" I asked. "I have seen several estimates, and I want to know which one is more likely to be correct."

"What have you heard?" he asked.

"I have seen $4 million, and I have seen $8.5 million," I answered.

"Four million is not correct," he said. "I know of loans in the amount of $6.2 million, and I know that Hardee's put equipment valued at over one million dollars inside the two restaurants they operated. That brings the estimate to $7.2 million, and there may have been more spent, as well."

"So, four million is too low," I said.

"Yes, four million is too low, and $8.5 million may be too high, but, it could have been $8.5 million by the time all the bills were paid," Jesse said.

"Who owned it after the fair was closed?" I asked.

"C.H. bought out some of the other owners, using a shell company," explained Jesse. "I know that
William Denton wanted out, but, Dr. Morris may have lost
money." "Did anyone ever make money on the Sunsphere?"
I asked.

"I do not think so," he answered.

"But, there were over 60,000 people per day paying $2 each for the six months of the fair," I said. "That would mean that approximately $18 million dollars was collected from ticket sales."

"All ticket sales and cash from concessions were carefully accounted for," said Jesse. "It was counted and distributed as was required by the agreement with KIEE."

"Then, if $18 million dollars was collected, it was used appropriately," I said.

"I do not know that $18 million dollars was collected from ticket sales at the Sunsphere," said Jesse Barr.

"Rumors continue to go around," I said.

"Whatever money was collected was put back into the fair to pay for things as they were needed each day," Jesse explained.

"The money collected was often used within the next week to keep things afloat," he explained.

"I nearly lost my mind juggling loans from one bank to the next. When Jake needed money, he might have had needed $25 million. It had to be found somewhere, and I was the guy on the phone looking for it. I spent many a sleepless night from 1981 to October 31, 1982. Then, the day after the fair when the federal regulators came into the banks in mass, I had even bigger troubles."

"Would it be safe to say that the Sunsphere and its future got lost in the shuffle of the collapse of the Butcher Banking Empire?" I asked.

"That would be the right way to put it," said Jesse. "The Sunsphere was not a priority."
(interview June 2007)

*Records show that the estimate of 60,000 people per day as paying $2 to see the Sunsphere was incorrect, making the figure of $18 million too large of an estimate as well.

Jesse Barr was 77 years old in 2014. He retired from Dean Stallings Ford when it closed.

Jesse Barr in 2008 in attendance at a luncheon held at the Sunsphere hosted by Martha Rose Woodward honoring Randy Tyree, Bill Denton, and Mr. Barr.
Photo by Barrett Buie.

1982
The world comes to Knoxville.

This book is not about the World's Fair, however, if there had not been a World's Fair there would not be a Sunsphere. Therefore, it would be almost impossible to write about the Sunsphere without also writing about the World's Fair.

The World's Fair was held for 184 days from May 1, 1982 until October 31, 1982. It has been called One Big Party. Reports at the time referred to when "The World Came to Knoxville". It was defined an official international exposition, fully licensed and sanctioned by the Bureau des Expositions Internationales in Paris, France. It was the first fair held in the southeastern United States in 97 years, and it turned out to be the next to last fair held, with the fair held in New Orleans in 1984 being the last one. The Fair was open daily from 10 a.m. until 10 p.m. with the amusement area often staying open until 1 a.m.

Tickets cost $9.95 for adults (12 to 54) $9.25 for seniors (55 and over) $8.25 for children (4-11), and free to children 3 and under. There were special discounts given to groups. Season passes and 2 day tickets were sold as well. The Fair was located on 72 acres between the campus of the University of Tennessee and the Tennessee River. It was bordered by Western Avenue, Henley Street, Neyland Drive, and 11th Street.

A committee named as an advisory board was formed in 1974 by Mayor Kyle Testerman, This group of businessmen was given the task of exploring the ideas of bringing an International Exposition to Knoxville. Mayor Testerman and other city officials, as well as businessmen had heard about the World's Fair which had been held in Spokane, Washington. That fair had helped that city with its urban renewal goals. The city of Spokane and Knoxville were about the same size, the population was nearly the same and both were located within driving distance of other major cities and points of interest.

When Randy Tyree was elected and came to office as mayor, many plans had already been set into motion for the fair. It was hoped that the fair could be held in 1980, but securing the financing, and fighting the local citizens who did not want a fair if it would force an increase in taxes, proved to slow down the progress of the fair. The 1980 date was moved forward to 1982. The advisory board of Mayor Testerman was renamed as Knoxville International Energy Exposition. Bo Roberts was named as president of the committee, with Jake Butcher named as chairman. The catchy phrase of "Expo '82" became the rallying call for the KIEE Board.

During the decade of the 1970s, energy was an issue that was in the forefront of everyone's mind. Citizens had spent long hours in line waiting to get enough gasoline in order to drive themselves back and forth to work. It seemed a natural fit for the city leaders to make energy the focus of the fair. They were hoping to introduce new sources of energy and new technologies to the public. Historically speaking, international expositions had been used as a way of getting new inventions and new products out to the masses. The members of the KIEE had big dreams of displaying the latest gizmos and gadgets which would spark the imaginations and interests of tourists. The new items which actually did debuted during the 1982
World's Fair were the flavor of Cherry Coke, boxed milk which will not spoil while sitting on the shelf unopened, touch screen monitors, and Petros' Chili and Chips. Petro's was a big hit by fairgoers, and continues to be in operation today.

The World's Fair was planned to include live entertainment, parades, displays, exhibits, musical and sporting events, food, costumes, rides, games, arcades, and more. There were numerous countries that had joined the KIEE as hosts. Each country built a pavilion and presented exhibits, entertainers, and gave out information. The nations who participated in the World's Fair were: the United States, Canada, Australia, West Germany, France, Hungarian People's Republic, China, Saudi Arabia, Italy, Great Britain, Belgium, The Netherlands, Denmark, Ireland, Luxembourg, Greece, Japan, Republic of Korea, Mexico, the Philippines, United Kingdom, and the European Community. In order to recruit each of these countries, the members of the KIEE spent hundreds of hours traveling and making phone calls. Landing the country of China was seen as their greatest accomplishment.

Not only were events scheduled on the fair site, but off site as well. Performances by Bob Hope

and Charlie Pride drew the largest crowds. Another high point for the citizens of Knoxville and Knox County occurred during a week in October when the football team of the University of Tennessee defeated Alabama for the first time in 11 years.
(interview with Randy Tyree 2007)

Knoxville's 1982 World's Fair Images of America published by Arcadia Publishing in South Carolina in 2009 was written by Martha Rose Woodward.

1982   May Day May Day

   With landscapers, construction workers, painters, vendors, and more working late into the night, the days and nights before May first were a hectic and fearful time for everyone. Many local people who had voiced their opposition to the fair were certain that the fair site would not be ready for the opening day. Members of the local, state, and national media began reporting on the fair, and even with all the negative attention it was getting, the 1982 Energy Exposition opened on a bright summer's day with President Ronald Reagan giving the opening speech.

   To Jesse Barr, President Reagan's speech was a slam on former President Jimmy Carter.

   "Reagan was only there because he had to be," said Jesse Barr. "Remember, Jimmy Carter was the President who gave permission for the fair to take place. Reagan saw the fair as Carter's fair. Read his speech, Reagan made a point of attacking Carter's energy policies."

   It is a known fact that Reagan appeared under heavy security at the fair and was whisked away quickly for a visit to the home of then Senator Howard Baker. Reagan did not take the time to tour the Sunsphere, although he certainly saw it while he was making his speech. Reagan's speech is reprinted here in its entirety. The reader can decide if Jesse Barr's opinion was correct.

Preisdent Ronald Reagan:

May 1, 1982

Ladies and gentlemen, Your Governor, Senator Baker, Your Congressmen, members of our Cabinet, and a good friend and loyal Tennessean, Dinah Shore:

It's a special pleasure for me to be here this afternoon in the shadow of the Sunsphere, a symbol of energy potential, near the banks of the Tennessee River, whose force we have tapped for centuries.

All Americans can be proud of this World's Fair that we open today. For the next 6 months, we'll be host to representatives of 22 nations—more countries than have participated in any world exposition in more than a decade. Here in Knoxville, in the Tennessee foothills, in the hometown of John Duncan, the home State of my good friends Howard Baker and Lamar Alexander, Robin Beard, and Jimmy Quillen, the world will share its knowledge, accomplishments, and hopes for tomorrow. Americans welcome the world to Tennessee.

The technology exhibited here once seemed as fanciful as the extraction of sunbeams from cucumbers in "Gulliver's Travels". But as de Tocqueville said, when people live in democracy, enlightenment, and freedom, their societies will be marked by scientific genius and discovery.

The countries represented here hold out the hands of friendship and cooperation; let us join them. Inventors of the world share the discoveries of their laboratories, universities, and research centers; let us pool our knowledge, technology, and our dreams. In the days and months ahead, let this spot be the focus of progress, not only in the field of energy but for the cause of peace.

The theme of this fair, "energy turns the world," is appropriate for this decade, as our nation and many of our allies struggle to produce and use energy efficiently—to provide for our energy security.

We've seen the havoc and felt the pain brought on when vital energy sources outside our influence have been cut off. We've seen our economies manipulated, our industries hamstrung, and our people squeezed between scarcity and inflation. Together and independently, we've taken steps to make sure that never again will we be so vulnerable.

Here in America, in this administration, our national energy policy dictates that one of the government's chief energy roles is to guard against sudden interruptions of energy supplies. In the past, we tried to manage a shortage by interfering with the market process. The results were gal lines, bottlenecks, and bureaucracy. A newly created Department of energy passed more regulations, hired more bureaucrats, raised taxes, and spent much more money, and it didn't produce a single drop of oil. In fact, American oil production continued to decline. Just as in today—and too many other cases—government did not solve the problem; it became the problems.

Our administration is determined to press forward for real solutions. Already we have dramatically increased our Strategic Petroleum Reserve. Instead of managing scarcity, we'll help ensure continued supplies from a strategic stockpile, alleviating shortages while permitting the private market to work.

Our stockpile, I'm happy to tell you, is now one of the largest in the world—more than a quarter billion barrels—an amount greater than 135 days' supply of the crude oil we import from the Arab OPEC nations. Last year, this reserve has been stocked with more than twice as much oil as was accumulated in the preceding 4 years. We will increase it to nearly three times our current supply as a symbol to our allies of our resolve to reduce our vulnerability. We will ensure that our people and our economy are never again held hostage by the whim of any country or cartel.

In the area of conservation, our industries and our citizens have increased energy efficiency and cut back on waste. The amount of goods and services that we produce for each unit of energy went up last year by 4 and one half percent—the greatest increase in 30 years. For the last several months, our net oil imports have been less than half of their 1977 levels. But energy is still a great concern. Even with our improved conservation, we consume 16 million barrels of oil a day.

Now let me give you an example of how many 16 million barrels is. Imagine the distance to the Moon. If those 16 million barrels were stacked up each day, they'd reach the moon about once a month. We're the world's largest consumer of energy. But we use that energy well.

We are one of the most productive nations in the world. Estimates show that the 25 eastern States and Washington, D.C. –which depends most of its energy shuffling paper—produce about as much in goods and services as the entire Soviet Union. And with only 5 percent of the world's population, we Americans account for more than 21 percent of the world's output. But we can't afford to be complacent. Our energy appetite means our energy production must be allowed to keep pace.

In the last year, our oil production in the lower 48 States ended its decades-long decline. In 1981 America produced nearly 90 percent of the energy that is consumed. What caused this turnaround? The same principle responsible for most of the prosperity, production, and progress in the world today: free enterprise.

Our economic and energy problems were in large part caused by government excesses and quick fixes, not by a basic scarcity of supply. Our principles have not failed us. Too many times, we have failed to live up to our principles.

Since January 1981, when I ordered immediate decontrol of oil, we have removed requirements for more than a million man-hours of energy-related paperwork, eliminated more than 200 energy-related regulations, cut taxes to encourage capital investment, begun to dismantle the Department of Energy, and reduced spending nearly $5 billion from the levels proposed by the previous administration. We're unleashing, again, the power of our people and the forces of democratic capitalism.

Skeptics said the decontrol of oil would send prices soaring. But the price of gas at the pumps has been dropping. Gasoline prices, at last, no longer lead inflation but are actually holding it down. Within a year of decontrol, more than 1,000 new drilling rigs began searching for oil and natural gas. Forty percent more successful oil wells were completed in 1981 than the year before. In February our oil production was the greatest it's been for the last 2 years. There is magic in the free marketplace, and it works.

Although oil has been decontrolled, natural gas, the nation's largest source of domestic energy production, remains under price controls. As a result, natural gas wells have increased only 10 percent. The legislative agenda this year is too crowded to handle the issue of natural gas decontrol. But if America is too provide for her energy security, if we're to continue growing more self-reliant, if we're to free ourselves from foreign pressure, we must press toward the ultimate solution to our energy problems; the decontrol of all of our energy sources, including natural gas. And this we shall do.

Within our boundaries and just off our shores, experts estimate that compared to our current reserves, three times as much oil and gas our yet to be discovered. We're also blessed with a quarter of the free world's coal and uranium resources.

In the last year, America has also greatly increased exports of coal; strengthening our economy and helping our allies lessen their dependence on imported oil. In 1981 exports from this country of coal reached 110 million tons. That's 20 percent more than the previous year.

Coupled with our decreasing oil imports, this meant America's net dependence on foreign energy fell to less than 13 percent. It was nearly 25 percent in 1977.

Though quite small, our use of solar power is expanding. Many people across the country are experimenting with renewable technologies such as wind and geothermal power. The Synthetic Fuels Corporation has also become operational, managing loan guarantees and price supports for some important projects. But heavy reliance on these sources is still in the future. We still have to depend on practical sources available today, such as nuclear power, which now produces more of America's electricity than oil. The Clinch River reactor, which will use new breeder technology, and the Oak ridge National laboratory, not far from here, symbolize our commitment to developing safe nuclear energy and technology to secure our energy future.

Our Secretary of Energy, Jim Edwards, tells the story about the time in his home state of South Carolina he spotted a car bearing a bumper sticker, "Split wood, not atoms." Wee, he said he didn't think the fellow driving the car had ever split much wood-especially not a one, enough for a typical family's needs— because it isn't very easy. I can testify to that. But Jim said he wanted to tell him that America must split both atoms and wood. It'll take the use of many technologies to satisfy our future energy demands.

We're pursuing our goal of energy security while still respecting and protecting our environment. The staggering statistics of progress that I've recited today—our growing independence from foreign oil and our increasing sophistication in using our reserves—reflect American ingenuity at its best. This progress didn't come about as the result of some government program. It's the result of getting government out of the way.

We're applying the same philosophy to our economy; restoring incentive, rewarding risk taking and hard work, encouraging investment, and returning more freedom to the marketplace. An economic, mess has been piling up for more than 40 years. Our economic recovery program began only 6 months ago, but already there are visible signs of success.

In the last 6 months, inflation, which was 12.4 percent, has been running at a rate of only 3.2 percent. And last month the consumer Price Index—the measure of inflation—actually went down. For the first time in 17 years, not only did goods not get more expensive; they got cheaper. In the 6 months since our tax cut took effect, the rate of personal savings has increased. And we've seen recent gains in housing starts, auto sales, and retail sales.

Now, we still have a long way to go before our economy is back in shape. And this recession is causing great pain to too many of our people. But there was a thing called the Misery Index that was created in the 1975 Presidential campaign. It was used against the then incumbent President Ford. And the misery index had been created by adding the rate of inflation and unemployment. And at that time, they were something around 12 percent. And they were used over and over against, as I say, the President in that campaign. Well, in the 1980 campaign, they didn't mention the misery index, because it had risen to 20.8 percent. I'm happy to tell you that the misery index is now currently 9.8 percent.

Still, there is pressure from many sides to retreat to business-as-usual. There are still those in leadership positions who would allow government to grow bigger and bigger. Many well-intentioned people suggest that we can't spend less and we must tax more. As the decisions become tougher and the stakes get higher, some people in Washington are throwing up their hands. Their only answer for our energy problems, for our economy, and for virtually any difficulty at all, is more government.

Well, we will continue to press for a bipartisan budget. But the only compromise offered so far has been: If our side agrees to raise taxes, the other side will continue to increase spending. You know, trying to end the recession or eliminate the deficit by raising taxes is like the Big Orange trying to pull a football game out in the fourth quarter by punting on third down. No government in the history of civilization has ever voluntarily reduced itself in size. But with God's help, this one's going to.

Yes, we had the largest tax cut in history last year, but it barely offsets the massive, largest tax increase in history that had been passed in 1977. And yes, we cut the rate of growth in government spending— nearly in half. But, if we don't cut spending more and if we don't protect the people's tax cut, we'll see the largest deficit and the highest personal tax burden in American history.

I don't believe that you sent us to Washington to raise your taxes. And I don't think you sent us to Washington just to do what everyone did before us—spend and spend and spent. We don't have a trillion- dollar debt because we don't tax enough; we have a trillion-dollar debt because we spent too much.

We must balance the budget but history shows it can't be done simply by raising taxes. And for that reason, I've asked Congress to pass as soon as possible a constitutional amendment to require a balanced budget. Then there will be no partisan pointing of fingers; there'll be no refusal to compromise; and there will no longer by any red ink below the bottom line of our budget.

Twenty years of tax-and-spent policies resulted in 21 percent interest rates, back-to-back years of double-digit inflation, and the unemployment rate that afflicts us today. Retreating to those tired old policies will only bring us more of the same. We plan to hold down spending, reduce taxes, and return prosperity. And we think that's the most compassionate program of help for the people that we can possibly produce.

I'm sure that patriots in every country believe that their nation holds the key to world progress. But I have long believed the United States of America and her people have a special destiny. Abraham Lincoln said, "God would never cease to call America to her true service, not only for her sake, but for the sake of the world. " I believe the challenge of this generation of Americans is to turn our country to a different path, to restore it to the principles that made it great, because the free world—indeed, western civilization—needs a strong United States.

The community of nations must work together to achieve stability, security, and peace. This exposition that we open today is another step toward achieving those goals.

You know, to those who have refused to take part, who are conspicuously absent, who continue to lock their people in misery through isolation and tyranny, we can say to them only: We wish you had come. But we'll make no effort to hide this wealth of ideas. We believe advances in the human condition can only come from open markets, free trading, and stiff competition. Men and nations who ignore those forces will be lost to time.

Let the rest of us draw from this exposition a sense of confidence and community. Let us realize that free men and women still have the power to better their lives and raise the standard of living for all mankind. Let us recognize that those things that bind us and keep us strong; our democratic political institutions, our market economic systems, our commitment to liberty, and our belief and faith in human dignity. And let us reaffirm our partnership among citizens, among States, and among nations.

What a partnership it was for this community to bring forth this great exposition. Maybe we should all recall that late in the last century, there was a great world exposition. And, at that time, there was a Member of our Congress who actually proposed a measure to eliminate the Patent

Office, because he said that everything had been invented that needed to be invented or that could be invented. Well, I wouldn't be talking into a microphone today, if we'd gone along with that.

As we pool knowledge and resources here in Knoxville, our cooperation will become the keystone of a more peaceful and stable world. And now, I 'm looking forward to seeing something of this exposition. Thank you all. Have a good time, and God bless you.

The President spoke at 12:33 p.m. in the Court of Flags on the World's Fair site.

Photo from 1982 World's Fair Guidebook courtesy of KIEE.

1982   Gunshot breaks window pane

Not every citizen in Knoxville and Knox County was in favor of the World's Fair. Many people wanted the issue to come before the voters so that citizens could demonstrate their support, or lack of it. The most vocal group, Citizens for a Better Knoxville, which was led by Joe Dodd, a University of Tennessee associate professor of political science, and Leon Ridenour, held rallies and gave interviews with the local media. However, the plan for the Fair was never put forward on a referendum for a vote by the citizens. At the time, many people felt that the World's Fair was thrust upon the city, whether the people supported it or not. Tempers were short, many people were outraged, but the Knoxville International Energy Exposition Board plowed forward, hell bent on having "their fair."

The Sunsphere was built amidst this controversy. There were heated letters sent to the editor of the local newspaper, law suits were filed, while the air waves of the local radio stations were filled with angry voices complaining about the financial burden the City was taking on in the name of its citizens. Many people felt certain that the taxpayers would be left holding a bag of bills, and would not have anything to show for their hard work. Under the leadership of Mayor

Randy Tyree, a Democrat who had defeated the former mayor, Kyle Testerman, and with the persuasive ways of Jake Butcher and Jesse Barr, the plans for the fair continued, and steamrolled forward.

One early morning in May, a gunshot rang out and one of the golden glass window panes of the Sunsphere was shattered. Although no one was ever arrested for the incident, it seemed to express the frustration of the local citizens who were already hearing rumors of cost overruns and mounting debts surrounding the construction going on at the fair site. This would be the first of only two times in which one of the golden windows was broken. (interview Park Patrol, June 2007)

1982 Temporary friends

Hardee's Fast Food Restaurant built a temporary restaurant on level 1. This part of the structure has long since been removed.

Large yellow tents were also used to reduce the heat which reflected up from the sidewalks and was one of the major concerns during the summer months of the Fair.

Documents found in the Office of the Register of Deeds which were filed on March 17, 1982 state: "a temporary facility and/or structure for use by the Grantee (which was Hardee's) and his licensees as a temporary structure to house a fast food restaurant".

It also says, "…after completion of the 1982 World's Fair, the Grantee shall immediately, at its own cost, thereafter restore the Owner's Property to the same condition in which it existed immediately prior to the construction of the temporary building structure, grass, trees, shrubs, flowers and other plantings and all sidewalks, parking areas, paving, curbing and other improvements" (Siler, Charles, 12-3-81)

1982-1984
Sunsphere Restaurants:
The blue room, and more…

There were two restaurants located in the Sunsphere. Hardee's Fast Food Restaurant was housed on Level 1 which is ground level. There was actually a separate, temporary structure and several bright yellow tents built on the ground and attached to the base of the Sunsphere during the six months that the fair was in operation. There were picnic tables and chairs installed to handle the large crowds.

The Sunsphere Restaurant was located on levels 5 to 8. Level 5 is where most of the restaurant equipment was installed for use by the Sunsphere Restaurant. This restaurant was planned as a site for fine dining.

Level 5 is also the location of the Blue Room, which featured mirrored walls covered with blue velvet. The Blue Room, which seated 38, was referred to as VIP and also Executive Dining during the World's Fair. Diners who used the Blue Room were asked to wear semi-formal attire, with a coat and tie being required by the gentlemen. Tables in the Blue Room were set with crystal, silver and white china, as well as being covered with white damask cloths. For much of the time, Ronnie Wyche, professionally, known as Reginald, was the maitre d' in the Blue Room. Table-side cooking was provided, and added flair to the chic atmosphere.

The Blue Room was not used by most people who attended the fair. It was used by the Butchers, city and county officials, and friends of Jake, as their own personal dining space. Most people probably never even knew the Blue Room existed. Although it was a beautiful site which offered up-scaled and delicious food, the Blue Room was closed in 1984. There were mumblings of lack of space, high prices, lack of adequate parking, and the inability of the restaurant to keep employees as reasons as to why the Blue Room failed.

Level 6 inside the golden globe was said to be able to accommodate 120 diners, while Level 7 could seat 140. The price of meals ranged from $8.95 to $17.95. Liquor, wines, and beers were on the menu, as well as beef tenderloins, shrimp, prime rib, crab, game hens, and more.

Although levels 6 and 7 were not as posh as the Blue Room, these levels were decorated in styles that were in fashion at the time. Gold, green, and orange, as well as red were colors used inside the Sunsphere Restaurant. The architects who planned the Sunsphere had studied the sun, and had hoped to have white carpet on the inside of the ball, because the sun is said to be white inside. However, financial considerations put the damper on most of their ideas. Most decisions that were made came about because of the bottom line, which was money. "They did what they could afford," said William Denton. "Things were changed dramatically because of costs."

The managers and representatives for Hardee's Food Systems, Inc., of Rocky Mount, North Carolina were all smiles on February 28, 1982 as they viewed the plans for the two restaurants they would operate in the Sunsphere. They signed a 20 year lease for the space in the Sunsphere, but they were out of business by the end of 1984.

Those on hand for the announcement were: Al Weaver, general manager of the Sunsphere Restaurant; David Kennedy, director of special services, specialty food service division, Bob Sullivan, Hardee's director of development and the 1982 World's Fair project, Bill Holtzinger, director of operations for the Sunsphere, and Gene Arnold, president of the special food service division, along with Rolf Tinner, executive chef for the Sunsphere Restaurant.

Although Hardee's was successful during the six months the fair was in operation, smiles would fade to worries as the crowds dwindled, and so did their hopes of keeping their restaurants afloat. Hardee's gave the idea of having two restaurants their best shot, but after two years, they walked away from all investments in the building. (Knoxville News-Sentinel, Dec. 4, 1981, Charles Siler)

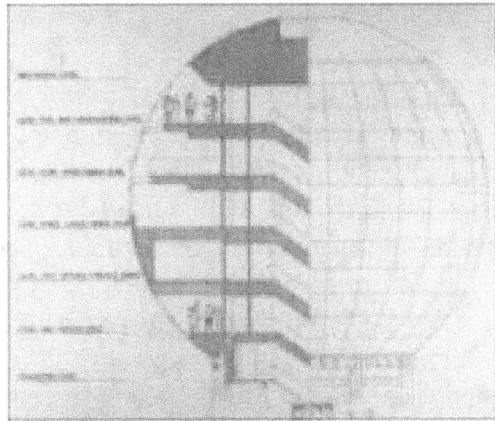

Diagram of inside the globe.

Facts: The Sunsphere is managed by the Public Building Authority, and is a part of World's Fair Park.

There are 3 elevators in the Sunsphere; two for passengers, one known as the service elevator. The round trip takes 3 minutes.

There are 8 levels. Levels one, two, and three are ground levels. Levels 4, 5, 6, 7, and 8 are in the golden ball.

Level 4 is known as the Observation Deck. It has a capacity of 68.

Level 5 contains kitchen equipment left by Hardee's. It was previously home to the Blue Room, and contained blue velvet on the mirrored framed walls until 2009.

Level 6 is said to truly give the best view since the windows are flat. It was used for the Sunsphere Restaurant and held approximately 130 people.

Level 7 was used as office space and dining.

Level 8 was previously home to more Observation.

There are 2 restrooms on each floor in the golden ball, and two on level 3. The tower is 192 ft. while the ball is 74 ft., making a total of 266 ft.

It took over 15 months to build the entire structure.

Community Tectonics was the architectural firm that designed it

Rentenbach was the General Contractors.

Stan Lindsey of Nashville was Consulting Structural Engineers.

West, Norris, Welch and Miller were the Consulting Electrical & Mechanical Engineers.

Bells

Jesse Barr remembers the bells which were installed in the Sunsphere. He loved them and was interested to know if the bell system was still in existence.

A 246 Bell Maas-Rowe Carillon was installed for the World's Fair. For the tower, Maas-Rowe provided 1,000 watts of solid state amplification and sixteen 6-1/2' air column speakers to project the sound. The bells make sounds by causing metal to strike metal in order to generate the tone. The music can be played from a console as well as automatically at scheduled times. The chimes ring on the hours, and can be scheduled for half or quarter hour, once per day, or week, as well. The sounds of the bells could be heard for more than a mile away, without being too loud near the tower. The bells were not used for a period of years, but were heard in 2003. Maas-Rowe Carillons, Inc. is located in Escondido, California.

According to park employees, as the years passed by, the loud speakers and other parts of the systems which operated the bells, simply wore out. The huge expense to replace the equipment or to buy a new system was more than the budget of the World's Fair Park could afford.

When the Sunsphere reopened in 2007, the bell system was encased in a glass cabinet. Plans have been made to remove the bell system in 2014. (www.maasrowe.com/EXPO.html) As of 2014 plans were laid to remove the entire bell system.

June 1982   William Denton sells his part of the Sunsphere to C.H. Butcher.

It is not typical for an architectural firm to own the building it is going to build, however, in order to help the city and promote the fair, William Denton had signed his name on a $1 million dollar bank loan in order to make the Sunsphere come to a reality. In June 1982, William Denton sold his part of the Sunsphere to C.H. Butcher. Mr. Denton thinks that he was well paid and he was glad to be out of the deal. He was grateful for the opportunity to work on the unique structure. He looks back at those days as a special time full of hope for the future. He enjoyed his participation on the Sunsphere and he is glad that he had the opportunity to build it. The time was right in June 1982 and he sold out, and he made a profit. (interview July 2007

November 1, 1982   The Party is over.

The six months of partying was over. On the morning of November 1st, 1982, architect Don Shell, arrived for work as usual only to find that his office which was located in the United American Bank Building on Gay St. in Downtown, Knoxville was closed. He had been locked out by the federal regulators who were busy examining the bank's records. Mr. Shell and others were in shock as they begin to hear rumors about wrong doing involving Jake Butcher and his friends.

"We were not even allowed to go inside and get personal items," said Mr. Shell. "Things were taken out of our offices that we never saw again."

If people thought that November 1st was bad, they could not have possibly predicted the troubles they would face as the next few years would become a nightmare for Community Tectonics, the Butcher family, Butcher's friends and business associates as well as the City of Knoxville and many citizens of Knox County. (interview June 2007)

What began on November 1, 1982 would come to a culmination on Valentine's Day of 1983 when it would be determined that Jake Butcher was bankrupt. His flagship bank, The United American Bank which was housed in the skyscraper with the reflective windows on Gay Street was padlocked shut, taking the hopes and dreams of many people down with it. Jake Butcher had taken a banking empire which was in solid financial shape and made it worthless. It would be shown later that Jake, his family, and his friends had taken out 70 loans which totaled more than $211 million dollars. Sorting through the tangled mess would be described by one federal regulator as "like sorting through spaghetti in a can." One of Jake's secretaries said of him, "To Jake making a million or borrowing a million was all the same." (BMBT; Knoxville Journal, 11-83)

Jake's appetite for high living, his personal helicopter, as well as the airplane which stood on ready to whisk him away to an important meeting, were all gone. No wonder it was reported by many people who worked on the fairgrounds during the six months of the World's Fair that cash from the fair site was hauled into Jake's office in wheel barrels. It would be discovered that Jake's personal finances were in trouble during the six months the Fair was in operation and, in his mind, he saw the daily cash flow from the fair as something he needed in order to personally stay afloat.

The money being spent by the visitors to the World's Fair which was supposed to go to pay off loans and be paid as profit to people who had hoped to sell food, souvenirs, and tickets to rides, was, mostly, going to Jake. Although when asked what he had made from the World's Fair, Jake replied, "Not one single dime." Individuals who worked in the fairgrounds frequently said that the cash money from the Caribbean Bar, as well as from other places in the fair, went straight to Jake's office at the close of business each day.

One report said that "Jake has promoted, finagled, twisted, pushed, tugged, and worked for 5 years to make the World's Fair a reality." It appears from the information that came to light during the following years that Jake was motivated by greed not love for the city and its people. (BMBT; Knoxville Journal, 1983)

Randy Tyree, left, Jake Butcher, center, Bo Roberts, right, toast the ending of the 1982 World's Fair on Halloween Eve 1982. On November 1, 1982 bank regulators arrived to inspect the records of all of Butcher's banks by closing them and locking the employees and Butcher out. The largest case of fraud to ever hit the USA at that time was to be uncovered. By the time the dust was settled Butcher was found guilty of fraud and sent to prison for 7 years. Photo courtesy of KIEE.

December 1982

Xanadu Light Show

The Sunsphere Restaurant, which was located inside the golden ball, on levels 5, 6, 7, and 8 stayed open after the World's Fair was over. In 1982, after the fair had closed, the management of the restaurant used a light show to attract customers. The Xanadu light show, which gave the Sunsphere the appearance of revolving, led to many people believing that the golden ball did revolve. If the architects had been given the money, they could have made some of the levels of the globe revolve. But, staying within the budget they had been given kept them from including this in the plans.

The Space Needle located in Seattle, Washington does revolve, however. (advertisement Knox-News Sentinel, Knoxville, TN,12-6-82).

October 1982
Fire Sales

As the World's Fair was closing down, a host of fire sales were being held around town in which equipment, decorations, memorabilia, and more were sold. The pavilions of the twenty-two countries who were involved in the fair were dismantled and sold as scrap. Signs, flags, furniture, t-shirts, all sorts of souvenirs and even paper towels and toilet paper were seen at make-shift yard sales as vendors were hoping to recover some of their investments. At one final auction, everything including bricks, except the Amphitheatre, The U.S. Pavilion, and the Sunsphere were sold. It was as if the citizens wanted to wipe the slate clean from the World's Fair. Although the city has looked back at the World's Fair with loving eyes, during those times, there was a lot of bitterness and there were many unanswered questions. The vendors, the businesses, and the city needed every penny that could be made from the sales, and would also need more.

What was happening to the Sunsphere during all that time? For the most part, the Sunsphere continued to be a popular spot. Tourists enjoyed riding the glass elevators up for 192 feet to view the city scape.

Hardee's Restaurant continued to serve Sunburgers and Sunburst drinks. The Executive Dining Room continued to host customers.

Knoxville's City Council and Knox County's Commission wrestled with the bills from the World's Fair that continued to come due. Finances were in a state of flux with most people not knowing what could happen. In general, the fair had not performed at the level that had been predicted. Many people, who had entered into the last six months with high hopes of making big money, had seen their hopes dashed. Some people actually claimed to have made money. The fair had experiences high numbers in attendance, with the total of over eleven million visitors crossing the turn stiles, however, the city officials were asking,

"Where's the money?"

As it was pointed out, the eleven million who were counted as having visited the fair were not all paying customers. The staff, entertainers, the press, delivery personnel, and anything that went through those turn stiles was counted in the final totals. Considering the price of tickets alone, over eleven million visitors should have generated between $50 and $100 million dollars. The City had taken out a bond of $45 million dollars. Many were asking, "What did we get for all that money?"

Jake Butcher made a flamboyant and public display of gathering a group together in order to burn the loans which, he claimed, financed the World's Fair. He announced $30 million dollars in loans were paid, however, by this time, people in the City of Knoxville did not trust Jake. Whether they knew it or not, the citizens of Knoxville would be paying on that debt until May 2007. (personally witnessed)

1983   Look who's back?

Kyle Testerman was elected in 1983 and took office as Mayor in 1984.

Although Kyle Testerman was the mayor in 1974 who had appointed Jake Butcher to work on the feasibility study concerning the possibilities of bringing a World's Fair to Knoxville, it was Randy Tyree, a Democrat, who the voters blamed for the Butcher Scandal. Many citizens also resented the fact that Randy Tyree ran for Governor in 1978. The climate in Knoxville during 1983 was more that of a small town, rural attitude than one of a big city.

"Randy got too big for his britches," was the sort of comment heard throughout the town in barbershops and at the local restaurants.

People, who had elected Randy Tyree in 1973 by a slim margin of 350 votes of the 50,350 votes cast, and had re-elected him in 1975, were angered that the local mayor ran for the state-wide office. Randy Tyree decided that he would not run for a third term, opening the door for the Republicans to take back the mayor's chair. Many people thought that the vote for Kyle Testerman in 1983 was a vote against Jake Butcher. Mayor Testerman won the election of 1983 in the primary.

The city of Knoxville was in a state of flux caused by the Butcher Banking debacle. A firm hand was needed at the top. Kyle Testerman walked back into the mayor's office with his sleeves rolled up and methodically cleaned up. It is not difficult to see that Mayor Testerman worked tirelessly to help the city out of some touchy situations. Many citizens have told me that this city owes the former Mayor a huge debt of gratitude. He was the right person at the right time, and he did a great job.

1983   Arts Council uses space to display art work.

After the World's Fair closed, space in the Sunsphere was used for displaying the art of various artists by the Arts Council, a 501 3C group which promotes such things as ballet, painting, theater, museums, live performances, and more. It was a sort of a make shift museum for a while, displaying items from the pavilions which had been such an integral part of the fair and providing an opportunity for artists to show their work. Various individuals who recognized the historical value of items from the fair, saved, rescued, and preserved them. Hundreds of types of products were produced to be sold during the fair, and examples of them were kept and displayed. Many of those same items are a part of the exhibit which has been on display at the East Tennessee History Center on Gay Street in downtown, Knoxville.

Left over souvenirs and other things were sold from the site, too. (Personally witnessed)

1983 Elevator Door Stuck

Although there have never been any major accidents in the life of the Sunsphere, there was an uncomfortable incident that occurred in March of 1983. While touring the Sunsphere on a Sunday afternoon in early March, 9 people were trapped in the elevator for over three hours. They were rescued when they made a phone call from inside the elevator and were able to contact a telephone operator named, Polly Dawson, who called Montgomery Elevator Company, who sent a repairman to the Sunsphere within ten minutes.

It was thought that the elevators were sent off their route by winds which had gusted up to 40 M.P.H. on that day.

Polly Dawson was called a heroine, while the 19 year old student, Anita Martin, who was the elevator operator, was also praised. After the 9 people were rescued, they were given a free pass to ride the elevator once again.

1983 The Fall of the House of Butcher

In November of 1983, The Knoxville Journal Newspaper, a publication which used to be the second daily newspaper in Knoxville, commissioned a group of reporters to write about the Butcher Banking Scandal. The paper published a book which included stories and photographs, along with diagrams and copies of court documents detailing the lives of the Butcher family as they traveled from Union County to Knoxville, creating an empire by owning over 17 banks, real estate, air planes, cars, buses, and mansions.

This book has been out of print for many years, however, an individual who wanted me to get the true facts of the events which occurred during the years when the Butchers ruled Knoxville, loaned me a copy. I have read and reread the book until I almost wore out the pages. It remains an excellent source of information for anyone who wants to do more research about those times. It would be difficult to understand the atmosphere surrounding the Sunsphere in those times, without learning about that scandal.

In 2000, a writer from Oak Ridge, Sandra Lea, researched and produced a book in which she detailed the tangled and mixed up web of deceit which had been woven by the Butcher Brothers. Her book, *Whirlwind, The Butcher Banking Scandal,* is also an excellent account of the history of the Butchers.

The Butchers were Democrats. Whatever may be seen as their legacy, the fact remains, the only Democrat to be elected as Mayor of Knoxville from 1974 until 2011 was Randy Tyree.

The impact the Butchers had on the Sunsphere is clear. They wanted to use private and public funds to finance projects on which they could earn massive amounts of money. They saw the Sunsphere as a cash cow. They used it as if it were their private property and they hoped to position themselves to profit from any revenues it might bring in. At one point, it was believed that licensing and copyrights for all things having to do with the Sunsphere could be a highly profitable venture. There were estimates that elevators rides up to the observation deck could bring in hundreds of thousands of dollars, and the Butchers wanted to be involved in, what they thought would be, a steady stream of cash. However, when the fair closed, and the crowds dwindled, the amount of money being made dwindled as well. It was typical of the Butchers to stay with a deal until it no longer made money, and to bail out, leaving others to pick up the pieces. The financial deals surrounding the Sunsphere were just another part of a broken promises and broken dreams brought on by the Butcher Brothers.

The good people who worked on this building had no idea of the things that were going on concerning the Sunsphere and the Butchers. Many people felt lucky that they were not brought down with the Butchers. (Knoxville Journal 1983)

1984 Lawsuit Claims Sunsphere Design Copied from Mark Cardoso

The lawsuit filed by Mark Cardoso was settled in 1984 when the 3 judge panel ruled against Mr. Cardoso's claims. Mr. Cardoso presented evidence that he had met with Bo Roberts in 197 7 showing his ideas for a "tower of power," which Mr. Cardoso had protected under copyright laws. Mr. Roberts did share the ideas with the KIEE committee, but the ideas had been rejected. Mr. Cardoso claimed that the ideas which eventually became the Sunsphere came from his copyrighted plans. Mr. Cardoso sued KIEE . U.S. District Judge Robert Taylor had ruled against Mr. Cardoso by saying that the two designs were not that similar. The case was appealed to the 6th U.S.Circuit Court of Appeals in Cincinatti, Ohio. After hearing both sides, and viewing Mr. Cardoso's plans, the judges ruled against Mr. Cardoso, upholding the ruling of U.S. District Judge Robert Taylor

The "tower of power" could be said to be similar to the Sunsphere, in that both were towers, but the overall appearance of Mr. Cardoso's tower did not meet the "preponderance of evidence" requirements for the lawsuit. (Knoxville News-Sentinel, July 13, 1984, AP)
1984

Hubert Bebb, dead of gunshot wound

The citizens of Knox County awoke on an autumn day in October of 1984 to the news of the sudden and shocking death of architect, Hubert Bebb, age 81. Because of strict copyright rules, I cannot reprint the entire article from the local newspaper.

Mr. Bebb, (rhymes with web) had a life full of successes. He was a brilliant and talented architect, a businessman, and was much loved and admired by family and friends. Dealing with his death has been a difficult struggle for them.

Mr. Bebb first came to East Tennessee in the 1930s, having lived in Chicago, Illinois.
He felt inspired by the natural beauty of the area. He moved to Gatlinburg in the late 1950's with his wife, Louisa; living on Buckhorn Road off U.S. 321. He established a firm, Bebb & Olsen, Architects and Engineers, in Gatlinburg, Tennessee in 1955. The firm would go through many changes, and eventually become known as Community Tectonics, Inc.

It was possible for investigators to determine what probably happened to Mr. Bebb on that October day in 1984. He was found at the base of the heliport on the top of the University Of Tennessee Hospital, having been shot in the head. The death was ruled as a suicide. According to friends of the family, Mr. Bebb left a note to his wife explaining that he felt as he was a burden to her because of his poor health. It was known that Mr. Bebb wanted his body to be donated to the University of Tennessee for medical research. It is thought that he drove himself to the heliport so that he would be found near the Research Center. Although this may have seemed like a good plan to the ailing architect, it turned out to be of no use because his body was not found for three days which was too late for his remains to be used for the purposes for which he had intended.

The news report from that time period states that, "Bebb left home about noon Tuesday. He left a note on the kitchen table saying he was going to see a doctor in Knoxville. When he did not return, the family began contacting his physicians, but none of them had seen him. He suffered from Parkinson's disease and had a pacemaker. He was carrying an oxygen tank in his car when left that morning." (Knoxville News Sentinel, Oct. 4, 1984)

This was a tragic ending to the life of a remarkable individual.

"We shape our buildings, and thereafter, they shape us." Winston Churchill

Four mayors of Knoxville gathered in 2009 for a service honoring them by having their photos hung in the gallery outside the mayor's office. Left to right Bill Haslam (now Governor of the state of Tennessee), Kyle Testerman (center at podium), Randy Tyree, and Victor Ashe. Photo by Martha Rose Woodward

1984

Kyle Testerman's vision

When the World's Fair closed and all the hoopla was over, the city was left with a variety of empty buildings, and a section of land that needed a new use. Mayor Kyle Testerman worked with the federal government to secure a grant of $1 million dollars in order to turn sections of the former fair site into a park. The mayor began making the area into a park on the part of the land near what was called the Waters of the World and the section where Fort Kid and the Victorian houses now sit.

There would be many days of frustration ahead for Mayor Testerman as he dealt with the aftermath of the problems left by the fall of the house of the Butchers. The city needed a strong leader to sift through the maze of deals and broken promises which had been left by the free-wheeling bankers who had used public money as if it were their own private ATM machine.

The Sunsphere continued to be privately owned in 1984, but the city was in the second position on the loans. The structure would eventually become a part of the World's Fair Park and it would see numerous tenants in its future.

The former mayor, who had a background in development, refused to approve of a deal with Fairfield Redevelopment which was a plan that would have built trendy condos on the former fair site. The mayor canned the deal with Fairfield in favor of his own plans. Many people believe this was one of the former Mayor Testerman's greatest errors.

1985 Testerman vs. Woodson

1985 brought reports of arguments between Mayor Kyle Testerman and Robert Woodson and his son, Robert Woodson III, over ownership and purchase price of the Sunsphere. Mr. Woodson was one of the original partners who had signed his name on loans in order to make the Sunsphere happen. After the fair closed, and once the Butcher Banking Empire had collapsed, all deals concerning the Sunsphere fell onto the shoulders of Mayor Kyle Testerman who previously had stepped forward to keep the Woodsons from losing their investments.

"We saved them, and now they are getting greedy," was the remark made by Mayor Testerman in January
1985.

Two feasibility studies had been made of the Sunsphere, looking at possible uses. In one study, Jeff Fletcher, a local real estate agent, estimated the structure to be worth $750,000 by comparing the Sunsphere to various restaurants near its locality. Hop Bailey had estimated the value to be at $800,000 when he was hired by the city to make an assessment.

First National Bank of Louisville, Kentucky held a $2 million dollar mortgage on the Sunsphere. The city was seeking a clear title to the property in order to move forward with redevelopment of the fair site. The bank was holding out for an amount nearer to the $2 million dollar mark. Mayor Testerman was not going to pay more than the value set forth by the assessment. The quarreling was finally settled, as the city of Knoxville bought the Sunsphere for $750,000.

"The Sunsphere was designed to be a theme structure, and to be used as an observation deck, and as a restaurant," said William Denton, the led architect who designed the structure. "The windows, which contain real gold dust, are worth more than $1 million."(Harris, R. 1985)

It does not change

As the outrage and activity were occurring concerning the Butcher Banking Scandal, the Sunsphere stood there. The cast of characters who were in charge of it changed, but it did not. It remained a steel tower, with golden windows. Over the years, people would come, and people would go, but the building would stand, and it would have needs.

The structure is consistent. No matter who has been in charge of it, and no matter what decision has made about it, it stands there, tall and serene, with windows that glisten in the sun. Birds fly by and many of them stop, poop, and roost. The low, lonely whistle of the train can be heard in the distance, and the grinding of gears and humming of motors is ever-present in its space. Rain, wind, and all sorts of weather conditions occur, but it remains the same, a calm, tall, and silent structure. As the clock ticks, it is as if a money meter is running. The Sunsphere absorbs dollars for utility bills, maintenance costs, repairs, renovations, and payroll which is paid to the personnel who guard and care for it.

1986   Life ain't been no golden stair (Langston Hughes)
Stair climbing

In 1986, a local radio station, WIMZ, hosted an event in which people could raise money by getting paid to walk up the 418 steps of the Sunsphere. "Climb to the Sun" Stair Climb had two honorary chairmen, Phil Williams & Colvin Idol both from WIMZ Radio 104. The event was organized to raise money for cystic fibrosis. People were encouraged to ask for sponsors who would pay $5, $10, or more for each step that was climbed. Prizes were given to those who raised the most money. The event was the brainchild of the Arts Council and was well attended. The Cystic Fibrosis organization made money on the project. It may have been held more than one year, but I did not find information for confirming that report. (entry form: Cystic Fibrosis Stair Climb, 10-26-86)

The golden globe photographed by Bill Cotter from Los Angeles, California in 2011.

1987 Arts Council

In an arrangement which was brokered by Mayor Kyle Testerman, the Arts Council signed a 5 year lease, for $1 per year for the space, according to the executive director of the Council during that time, Wanda Harding. The Arts Council used the space for an art gallery, community meeting room, office space for about 7 employees, and as a reception area for special events. It was hoped that the Dulin Art Gallery could be built near to the Sunsphere; however, this did not become a reality. As a part of the deal with the Arts Council, the city continued to pay the $2,000 to $4,000 monthly utility bill on the Sunsphere, or between $24,000 and $48,000 per year.

The Arts Council's planned to use the Fourth floor as a gallery and observation deck, the Fifth floor as Art Council board room, the Sixth floor as office operations for a staff of 7, the Seventh floor as visual arts gallery and community meeting room, and the Eighth floor as special events and reception room.

There was a period of years in which this arrangement had great success. The Sunsphere was used for wedding receptions with most of the food being catered for the events. It was also used for parties, meetings, and other kinds of receptions. There were fees charged for these uses, and the city did take in revenues for rental of the space.

As the years rolled by, various artists displayed their work in the Sunsphere. However, lack of wall space on which to display art work, and the monumental task of hauling crates, boxes, art work, and frames up the elevators, were impediments to using this type of building for these kinds of purposes. During 1987, the fair site had not been redeveloped. Finding a place to park as well as the general attitude at the time against going downtown were some of the problems encountered by the council. There were numerous wonderful events held during those years. Citizens enjoyed the parties, receptions, and displays of amazing art work. Growth in their programs and the need for more space were the reasons why the Arts Council moved out of the Sunsphere. (Kay, Paul, 1-27-87, Daily Beacon)

1987
World's Largest Jack-'o-lantern

During the Halloween season in 1987, the Arts Council was promoting a children's event they called Saturday Night at the Fair Site. Someone in the Council thought it would be fun to make the Sunsphere the largest jack-o'-lantern in the world for a few days that month. The WIVK Radio Station sponsored the event, and agreed to pay the costs for painting the Sunsphere to make it look like a pumpkin which had been carved for Halloween. The station also added its call letters to the face where the mouth was located. Children loved seeing the Sunsphere painted in this way, and everyone was enjoying the fun and interesting art work. However, city inspectors became concerned about the name of the Radio Station being painted on the Sunsphere, saying that this amounted to a sign, and city ordinances prevented buildings of that height from being used as a billboard. The vice-president of WIVK, at that time, was Bobby Denton. Mr. Denton said that the station had meant no harm and had paid for the temporary paint job in order to support the event for the Arts Council. The city ordered the sign removed, and it was washed off on November 6, 1987. (Knoxville News- Sentinel, Oct. 28, 1987, Tom Williams)

1988

Arts Council Continues Success

Clearly, the Arts Council, a non-profit organization that promotes the Arts, made a success of their 5 year lease. Reporting that approximately 40 people toured the Sunsphere each week, and using the space for offices, as well as displaying work done by local and regional artist were seen as accomplishments. The Council also rented the space on Level 8 to private individuals for parties, receptions, and other events. "It was heavily used," according to an official of the park.

As with most agencies who have been involved with the Sunsphere during the last 25 years, the needs of the Arts Council simply outgrew the amount of the available space. Growth is a good thing, but the Sunsphere simply does not have the sort of wall space available which is needed for displaying paintings and photography. The Arts Council eventually moved out of the Sunsphere, and is located on Gay Street which provides the adequate amount of display space that is needed for their exhibits.

Individuals who used the office space in the Sunsphere during those years have happy memories of those times. "The scenery is breath taking," said one former official. "You simply cannot believe how amazing it can be to see a storm form and move through."

1986   Ownership

Like many of the financial deals surrounding the 1982 World's Fair, the ownership of the Sunsphere was not clear. Having spent a long afternoon at the Register of Deeds Office, I can tell you that looking through the deeds and the financial arrangements seemed to be like playing pinball; one deal bounces off another, and that one off another, and everything seems to keep going around and around. A very kind lady, who works in the Office of the Register of Deeds told me that it appeared that somebody was trying to hide something. But, who and what will probably never be known.

Also, Jesse Barr explained that if the bank regulators had not arrived on November 1, 1982 to inspect all 17 of Jake's banks, most of the financial arrangements that became huge problems would have been settled, and no one would have lost money. However, the regulators found enough evidence to order the banks closed, and trust in Jake and C.H. Butcher was gone, as well. The web of financial deals which had included federal grants, state grants, and loans from individuals as well from corporations was tangled, at best. By the time 1986 rolled around, the Sunsphere's ownership, and, therefore, its future use was in question.

The typical citizen in the Knoxville community probably had never given much thought to the ownership of the Sunsphere, or how its ownership would affect its use. Most people only knew what they had read in the newspapers, and details were often sketchy, at best. As Sandra Lea explained in her book, *Whirlwind; the Butcher Banking Scandal,* the original deal included ownership by several partners. One of those partners was the First National Bank of Louisville, Kentucky.

In 1986, the First National Bank of Louisville, Kentucky continued to hold a loan on the Sunsphere. When the City of Knoxville decided to buy the Sunsphere, the bank wanted the full amount due on the loan, which was $2 million. Thinking that this amount was far too much, the city paid for the property to be assessed. The value of the Sunsphere was estimated to be $750,000. The bank did not agree with this assessment and ordered an assessment of its own, which valued the Sunsphere at $800,000. The two sides battled back and forth, with Mayor Kyle

Testerman doing the clean-up work with yet another issue concerning the World's Fair although it had been closed for over six years.

The negotiations were often brutal. The General Services Administration became involved, and wanted to require that the city pay the $2 million which was owed on the Sunsphere. This prompted Mayor Kyle Testerman to tell the City Council, "The land is worth more without the Sunsphere on it." His statement led to rumors that he wanted the Sunsphere to be torn down. This was just one of the numerous times that talk of tearing down the tower would be heard throughout the city.

It was reported that during the title search which was done on the Sunsphere, it was discovered that one of the steel girders and part of the base were actually on city property. Finally, the deal was done, and the City of Knoxville purchased the Sunsphere for $750,000. This would not be the only time the city would spend huge dollars on the structure. (Harris, R, 1985)

1987-1988 Victor Ashe

In 1988, a 43 year old Republican, Victor Ashe, took the seat behind the mayor's desk and would hold it for the next 16 years. When Mayor Ashe came into office, there had been quite a strain on the relationship between the mayor and the city council. Different areas of the city held on tightly to "the way we do things over here". Mayor Ashe soon learned that he was going to have to work on his interpersonal relationships as well as the issues at hand in order to move his agenda forward. By all accounts, Mayor Ashe did a good job; good enough to continue to get himself elected, and, in politics, that is as good as it gets.

Although the former mayor has his detractors, he was able to accomplish numerous things which took the small city of Knoxville progressively into the future.

Since the scope of this book is all things Sunsphere, I want to keep the focus on Mayor Ashe's service as it reflects the life of the Sunsphere. For one thing, Mayor Victor Ashe had a solid record of being in support of public parks, greenways, and providing recreational opportunities for the citizens of Knoxville. The Sunsphere is considered to be a part of the World's Fair Park and sits only a few feet away from the New Convention Center which is one of the former mayor's largest accomplishments. It is a fact that the new center has not performed as successfully as it was projected, but it remains a beautiful building with potential.

The Sunsphere had a variety of things to happen to it during the sixteen years in which Victor Ashe was mayor. It was closed in 1999 in order for the new convention center to be built. There are whispers that the Sunsphere was neglected. To be fair, it was clearly not a priority. Perhaps it was tolerated, but it was not emphasized. Luckily, it was not torn down, either.

The former mayor was appointed as Ambassador to Poland in 2003 and he continued to live there with his wife and two children when I was writing this book. I was able to contact him via e mail. He responded quickly to my letter and he gave me the following quotes:

"I am pleased the Sunsphere is operating again and open to the public. It is an icon on the Knoxville architectural landscape. It should always be with us and used.

The World's Fair was a great defining moment for Knoxville and former Mayor Randy Tyree should receive more credit for it than he does, along with Jack Sharp and Jean Teague who loyally backed it on City Council despite major opposition at the time. The World's Fair not only cleaned up a decaying area but gave Knoxville a broad view of the future and the world around us. It built self-confidence for our city which needed it badly at that time in our history." (e-mail, July,2007)

1990   Piano man

Shake, rattle, but do not roll off the top.

In 1990, a trio of musicians led by Jason D. Williams played rock music while standing on his head from on top of the globe of the 266 ft. tall Sunsphere. Williams, a piano player from Memphis, was joined by drummer Gary Rolison, also from Memphis, and bass player Mike Harber of Missouri. The three were taping a music video sponsored by Tennessee Illustrated Magazine and Whittles Communications. The stage on which the piano was set was built on the ground and moved to the top of the Sunsphere by helicopter. The taping of the video was also done from a helicopter as a part of the 1990 Festival on the

River. Williams was tethered by a steel cable to a round, wooden platform or stage which had been attached to the top of the globe. Jason Williams' style of piano playing was compared to like Fats Domino, Little Richard, and Jerry Lee Lewis. The performance was a huge hit with the crowd. This event continues to be one event that everyone remembers. (Kauffman, Betsy, 5-17-1990)

1990   Somebody to love me.

Once the Arts Council moved out of the Sunsphere, the reoccurring challenge of making the space useable once again came to the forefront. The Knox County Tourism Bureau was looking for a new home because the building on Henley Street, where they were housed, was going to be torn down to make room for the new Henley Street Connector. The Bureau hired the architectural firm of Ross-Fowler to do a feasibility study to determine the likelihood of using the Sunsphere as a permanent home. Ross-Fowler did not charge a fee for doing the study, but the agreement was made that they would be hired to do the work, if the Bureau decided to move into the Sunsphere. The Bureau was given the go ahead by the firm and moved into the facilities in May 1992

The Sunsphere sat empty during most of 1990, 1991, and until May 1992, except for the influx of workers who were doing the feasibility study and the renovations.

Once again, tax dollars were spent on the Sunsphere by the city and county and by other local agencies.*

*author's note: Doing research for this book has often been confusing. As I sifted through hundreds of articles which have been written about the Sunsphere during the last 25 years, I began to notice that various agencies are reported by different names. The agency referred to as Knox County Tourism Bureau is also referred to as Knoxville Welcome Center and Tourist Bureau, and has now become The Knoxville Sports and Tourism Alliance.

1991 Tornados

When representatives of the Pensacola Tornados were looking for a place to open as their headquarters, they expressed interest in the Sunsphere, because, as one spokesperson said, "What better place for basketball offices than a giant basketball in the sky." An agreement was never reached with this group. However, it is interesting to note that the Lady Basketball Hall of Fame is definitely a golden basketball in the sky.

1991 Blue skies, nothing but blue skies

In August 1991, or ten years after it had been built, the county and city governments approved nearly $1 million dollars in order to renovate the Sunsphere. It was during this time that the elevators were changed and enclosed. Many people who remember the Sunsphere before the vinyl siding was installed around the elevators were outraged by this modification. The contractors in charge of making the change used the materials that the government could afford, and that was that. Safety was a main issue as well.

"They would not put vinyl siding on the Eiffel Tower," said one
architect. "It's a red neck's idea of culture," said a citizen.

However, the elevators had developed a problem. For some reason, when the wind rose to 15 m.p.h., the elevators would shut down. This made the Sunsphere virtually unusable, therefore, something had to be done.

The Mayor's plan also called for painting the tower. It was during this year when the color of the tower was changed from blue to green. Changing the color of the tower has been a sore point for the architects who built the Sunsphere. The tower was originally painted blue because the architects wanted the golden globe to appear as if it were floating along in the sky. Community Tectonics had gone through over 14 colors of blue paint before deciding on one special color of blue. A city spokesperson who asked to remain unnamed told me that the city sought input from local architects who recommended the color change due to the colors of the greenery in World Fair Park. It is not known why the officials did not contact the original architects or refer to the original blueprints before making this change.

Enclosing elevators, preparing levels 6, 7 and 8 to be used for office space, and making level 3 ready for the Welcome Center were the items listed as those that were changed before the Knoxville Welcome Center and Visitor's Bureau could move in and occupy the space under a lease agreement with the city. The Bureau moved in May 1992, and kept offices there until 1999. (Reed, Vita, 4-9-1992)

Woodward's book is available at www.amazon.com or from the author at e mail Sunspherebook@aol.com

1992-1998 Howdy!

During the years of 1992 until 1998, the Sunsphere was used by the Knoxville Convention and Visitor's Bureau as a Welcome Center and for office space. The Welcome Center was on Level 3, which is the Clinch Avenue level, while Levels 7 and 8 were used for the offices of 13 employees.

The Executive Director of the Bureau during those years was Al Treadway. Teresa Hall was Administrative Assistant and Office Manager. She agreed to answer some questions about the day to day operations in the Sunsphere for that time period. Here is a summary of what Teresa Hall said:

We occupied the Sunsphere from May 1992 until January 1998. Thirteen people kept offices there with 2 employees referred to as "Visitor Information Specialists" manning the Welcome Center. The Sunsphere was completely remodeled for use as offices. Furniture and equipment was brought in by the Bureau, and some items were purchased new. There were a few leaks in the windows, which were repaired in a timely fashion. There was no snack bar or restaurant being used by the employees. There was never a wig shop located there. The freight elevators were used until the other two were updated and put back into operation. There were never any frightening or unusual occurrences. The general public was allowed to tour the Observation Deck on Level 4. There were no weddings held there in those years. There were several times in which birds were discovered inside levels 7 and 8. Park employees were called and would come and net the birds and carry them out. There were never any accidents or injuries reported. People enjoyed being in the offices. Some people reportedly became seasick when the building moved or swayed. We really loved watching the storms blow in from the west and the sun rise each morning in the east. This was truly a sight to behold!

1992 Has it really been 10 years?

Victor Ashe was mayor as Knoxville's citizens looked back ten years and remembered the 1982 World's Fair. There were theme parties and celebrations held by various groups.

The Knoxville Convention and Visitor's Bureau signed an 18 year lease to use three levels of the Sunsphere as office space. Levels 7 and 8 were used as office space. The Visitor's Center on the Clinch Avenue level allowed tourist to walk right into the Sunsphere and get information. Al Treadway, the Bureau's executive director, was quoted as saying that the Bureau would move in by April of 1992. Funding for the project came from the City of Knoxville, Knox County Commission, and the Tourist Bureau. Extensive renovations were done to the inside of the Sunsphere during this time. The actual date on which the Bureau moved in was May, 1992.

As 1992 rolled around Former Mayor Randy Tyree began to get calls from the media wanting to invite him to events which would celebrate the 10 Year Anniversary of the World's Fair. The former mayor has always been glad to remember those years. He thinks that history will be kind to him.

"What we did was a huge urban renewal project," he said. "The city needed to clean up some property and to do something about the roads and highways. That is what the World's Fair did for this city. We were able to get millions of dollars of federal and state grants that we would not have gotten if we had not pushed the Carter Administration for the help."

1993 Snow and Ice

When a major snow and ice storm hit the city of Knoxville in 1993, damage was done to the Sunsphere, especially by the ice. The Sunsphere has over 720 windows, 360 outer, which contain 14 carat gold dust, and 360 inner. The gold dust in the window panes is often reported to be 24 carat, however, William

Denton says that it is 14 carat gold. It is only to be expected that these windows are going to need maintenance. Such was the case in 1993 as the residents of the city shoveled snow and struggled to repair damages caused by the massive storm. Work crews were sent to the tower to assess damages and make the repairs. Work of any type to the Sunsphere always draws a crowd. To those of us who fear heights, it is frightening to see men as they are swinging from ropes 266 feet into the air. However, I have heard and read that the workers who do these kinds of jobs think nothing of it. Weather stripping was placed between the window panes and the window frames, repairing the leaky windows, which was a relief to the office workers inside.

The Sunsphere is managed by the Public Building Authority. Expenses relating to it are paid for out of that part of the city's budget. (12-1993, News Sentinel)

1994 Management

Jim Begalla, who was the manager of the World's Fair Park for sixteen years, retiring in 2000, reported that discussions were underway in March of 1994 with two restaurant owners who were looking into the possibility of operating restaurants in the Sunsphere. By October of 1994, Greg Tribble, of Louisiana, was asking for permission to rent the space in the Sunsphere for 120 days to see if he could make a success of a restaurant on one of the lower levels of the space, as well as a more upscale dining experience using two upper levels. There was difficulty using the equipment on level 5, however, since the fire marshal would not allow the kitchen to grill steaks and burgers. The kitchen could only be used for baking, not frying.

There was a time during the years in which Mr. Begalla worked for the city when exterior lights were used to enhance the lighting on the Sunsphere at night. The park employees used equipment which only cost about $2,500 in order to place high intensity lights on the Sunsphere and several other buildings in the former fair site. This lighting was a popular as well as beautiful idea which was enjoyed for several years.

He also remembers that one window pane shattered and had to be replaced during the 1990s. There did not seem to be any reason, other than weathering or age for the window pane to crumble, but it did. A new window was ordered and had to be produced according to specific requirements; this took several months.

The Sunsphere continued to be used by the Welcome Center and Tourist Bureau until it was closed in 1999 in order for the construction of the new convention center. By all accounts, the years the Welcome Center used the Sunsphere were successful.

1994 Two Restaurants

The World's Fair Development Committee reported in 1994 that there were offers by two businesses to open restaurants in the Sunsphere. CEB Enterprises brought forth a proposal to open a casual dining restaurant similar to the one in Dallas. They would name the restaurant World's Fare Restaurant. Cierra Restaurant Group also wanted to open a restaurant for "fine dining." Both offers were turned down. (Dean, Jacqueline,3-16-94)

1996 More leaks

Once again, in 1996, the windows of the Sunsphere were leaking. Superior Plumbers & Caulkers, owned by Rocky McBee, made the repairs after the Knoxville Convention and Visitor's Bureau had made the complaints. Having been built in 1981, the Sunsphere was 15 years old at that time.The Convention and Visitor's Bureau continued to maintain offices from the Sunsphere, having moved there in 1992.

1996 Bart on the Road

On March 31, 1996, episode 148 in season number 7 of the animated cartoon show, The Simpsons, aired a program entitled, "Bart on the Road." In this episode, Bart and his friends Milhouse and Nelson use a fake driver's license Bart made for himself to rent a car and drive to Knoxville, Tennessee because they have found a travel folder about the World's Fair. When they arrive in town, they find that the World's Fair was closed many years ago, and all they see is the Sunsphere and a wig shop.

Unfortunately, this negative depiction of Knoxville, Tennessee and the Sunsphere left an impression of the Sunsphere as a tired old monument that could easily be knocked over by backing into it with a car. Although many people found the show to be humorous, just as many people found it offensive.

First, there was never a wig shop located in the Sunsphere. Second, the Sunsphere would not be knocked over if one car ran into it. All that would happen if a car ran into the Sunsphere would be that the car would smash flat. Lastly, school students need to read real history instead of relying on a cartoon show for information.

It is known that Conan O'brien, who is one of the writers of some of the Simpsons' shows, did have relatives who lived in Knoxville. Perhaps Mr. O'brien has seen the Sunsphere, and was motivated by his experience. (www.tv.com/simpsons)

1997 Rumors

From time to time, citizens of Knoxville would hear rumors that the Sunsphere was going to be torn down. There were discussions by city officials that, possibly, the city could not afford the upkeep on the Sunsphere. It is difficult to pin down statements for any particular one person about these rumors, but as person who lived through the times, I plainly remember hearing that there was discussions involving tearing down the Sunsphere. Nothing ever came of the rumors, and like most rumors, all the talk was just that, talk.

1998 Last Tour of Sunsphere Before It Closed

A group of students from a leadership class in Bearden High School toured the Sunsphere and were told that they will be the last group to be allowed inside the Sunsphere until after the new convention center is built. My daughter, Toni Erin Penery was a part of that group. Those students were born in 1982

1999 Sunsphere is closed to the public
"You can see a lot just by looking." Yogi Bera

In 1999, due to the construction of the new convention center, the Sunsphere was closed to the public. It had been leased by the Knoxville's Welcome Center and Visitor's Bureau, and had seen a relatively good amount of success from 1993 until 1999. It was estimated that approximately 100,000 people visited it each year during those years. There were no major problems in the Sunsphere, other than normal wear and tear. No one has ever been injured and there are no records of anyone ever having an accident in or around the Sunsphere, other than the incident concerning the elevator which trapped nine people for three hours.

However, since 1999, when the City of Knoxville bought the lease from the KTB for $378,000, the Sunsphere has had no tenants. It has sat empty, except for the birds.

"Nothing much goes on," said one worker who did not want his name to be given.

"I have worked here over ten years," said another person, "and nothing much has gone on up there." "How often is the Sunsphere checked?" I asked.

"Two or three times a day," came the answer. "We check for fire, and, generally, for anything that might be out of order."

"Since September 1, 2001, we have been on special alert, so, we go up inside the Sunsphere several times a day," the worker explained.

"Do people often ask you to allow them to go inside?" I asked.

"Yes, and before the renovations started, people often got permission to go inside," he explained. "It has been more difficult for people to see inside since the construction started because of safety reasons." "Do you feel safe going up the elevators?" I asked.

"Sure," he said. "That tower is strong and solid. It is not going to go anywhere."

"Do you have any highlights from the last few years?" I asked.

"No, it is usually quiet around the Sunsphere. We expect things to change when the new tenants move in," he said.

"It was a busy place while the convention center was under construction," he added. "There were about 50 people who had offices out of it. They used all of the levels and were in and out all the time." "Did anyone live there?" I asked.

"No, I do not think anyone ever lived there. It was quiet at night," he explained.

"The construction company was going to bring in trailers, but they decided to use the Sunsphere for office space," he explained.

Sadly, those 50 workers did not take care of the space inside the Sunsphere. Eye witness accounts and photos will verify that it was, basically, trashed on the inside for several years after 1999. (Reed, Vita, 1992)

2000   Sandra Lea's book is published

Sow the wind, reap the whirlwind.
Whirlwind: The Butcher Banking Scandal

Sandra Lea, a writer from Oak Ridge, Tennessee published the book, *Whirlwind: The Butcher Banking Scandal,* in 2000. This 647 page book provides specific details of the people and events which led up to the collapse of the Butcher Banking Empire. One of the aspects of this scandal was the financing of the Sunsphere.

The following is an excerpt from her book; pages 82 to 84, in which she writes about the complicated deals which were put into place in order to make the Sunsphere a reality.

Whirlwind: The Butcher Banking Scandal by Sandra Lea
Chapter 6 Sunsphere

Towering over the Knoxville Fair site is the Sunsphere, Knoxville's version of the Eiffel tower, the theme structure of the 1904 Fair in Paris, the Space Needle of the 1962 Fair in Seattle, Washington, and the Tower of the Americas at San Antonia in 1968.

The Sunsphere is not the tallest theme structure, but its design is the Sunsphere's mark of distinction. As far as is known, it is the first spherical floor-by-floor building ever constructed.

Built as a monument to the sun, the golden globe rises 266 feet and perches on a 192-foot tower of blue steel. The sphere is plated with 720 pieces of glass containing 24-karat gold dust, which cost about $1,000 each. The gold color reduces the air conditioning needed, but the mirrored appearance from the outside is transparent inside so visitors can survey the city or view the Smoky Mountains, the Tennessee River, and the entire Fair site.

The $8.5 million Sunsphere is capped by an observation deck on the top floor and had an elite restaurant, operated by Hardee's Inc., on levels two and three, the kitchen and a 25 seat VIP dining area on the fourth floor and another deck on the bottom. After the Fair, the owners planned to turn the top level into a "VIP" cocktail lounge and expand the menus of the two restaurants.

William Denton, president of Community Tectonics, the architectural firm that designed Jake's Whirlwind mansion, designed the Sunsphere. Denton had carried the project in his hip pocket wince 1979 when officials of the Fair approached him with the idea. They felt the exposition needed a theme structure, a centerpiece for the World's Fair site.

Several months of brainstorming yielded all sorts of cartoonish sketches depicting a sphere sitting on a concrete base and hovering close to the ground instead of towering over the Second Creek valley. The designs were more elaborate at first, but the design had to be modified when construction costs were estimated at several million dollars more than the Sunsphere operation could recover.

"In the early stages, the sphere was 86.5 feet in diameter because the diameter of the sun is 865,000 miles. Every little decision we made was from what we learned in the encyclopedias and reference materials. Naturally, we were more thematic in the early stages than we are now," Bill Denton said.

To decrease the price tag, the owners scratched some of the theme ideas, and the diameter shrunk from 86.5 feet to 74 feet. Still, the real expense came from meeting building codes, which said the tower must be built of concrete, which is fire-resistive.

Denton believed, however, that building codes are written for standard building problems for schools, and office buildings. "They don't think about world's fairs, and they shouldn't have to."

Armed with that belief, Denton went before the Knoxville Board of Zoning Appeals in the summer of 1980 and argued that the tower should be made of steel which is less expensive than concrete. The board said OK, and the project was "go".

Construction began in January 1981. Like a model kit, they pieced together the tower with standard-sized steel beams purchased from a handbook. Included in the construction were safety features such as two fire exits and a sprinkling, smoke evacuation and communications system.

Financing came from a partnership formed of East Tennesseans, who landed a $5.2 million loan from a

Kentucky bank and a $1 million loan through a Federal urban Development Action Grant.

What was unknown at the time, but came to light in 1983 when the Sunsphere Inc. stopped making payments on the 41 million federal loan, was who made up the partnership of East Tennesseans. The question of ownership became important as city officials addressed the problem of responsibility for the

$130,000 in past due payments for 1983.

Robert L. "Bob" Woodson Jr., a LaFollette, Tennessee, grocer and a director at United American Bank, was listed as Sunsphere Inc. president. Yet, when asked in a Federal Court trial if he did own an interest in the Sunsphere, Woodson answered that he had a very small interest.

An indemnity agreement showed that banker C.H. butcher Jr. had a "beneficial interest in the stock" of the Sunsphere. The agreement that was signed by C.H., was between Butcher and Dr. Robert W. Morris Jr., a surgeon, and William S. Denton Jr., former president of Community Tectonics, the panoramic tower's designer. It was signed June 2, 1982, the same day that Morris, Denton and Bruce McCampbell Jr., a local businessman, sold their stock to Sara Tackett, wife of Arnold Tackett an assistant to Shirley butcher, and lawyer Lewis Howard as a trustee. Howard represented a trust established on May 27, 1982, for First Union Investments Inc., a financial-services company controlled by C.H. Butcher Jr. the trust was referred to in the stock purchase agreement.

In the agreement, C.H. pledges to be responsible for any claims, liabilities, demands and obligations arising out of the financing of the Sunsphere with First National Bank of Louisville. The bank had the first mortgage on the Sunsphere.

Jesse Barr said that Jake's United American Bank and C.H.'s City and County Bank of Knox County made it a practice to finance as many World's Fair deals as appearances would allow. The Sunsphere was the exception. The First National Bank of Louisville, Kentucky, put up more than 44 million because the Sunsphere partnership had too many connections to Butcher.

Denton, Morris, Woodson and his son, Robert "Rob" Woodson III, signed papers making personal guarantees in a financing package that included the Urban Development Action Grant and $45.1 million in Knox County industrial development bonds bought by the Louisville bank.

At one time, Knoxville lawyer Sidney Gilreath also owned stock in the corporation. McCampbell's share was in a side agreement with Morris. When Gilreath, Morris and Denton sold their stock, Bob Woodson said that he and Mrs. Tackett purchased the stock. What was not announced was that the stock sold by Morris, Denton and McCampbell was bought by Mrs. Tackett and Howard, as trustee.

This was confirmed by Morris, who also said he thought Howard's trust was for C.H.'s son, butch. Sara Tackett's husband, Arnold, was also a Butcher associate.

One former stockholder said he had the impression that offers were made to purchase Gilreath, Morris and Denton stock because "they (Butcher and associates) wanted everyone else out."

Records with the Secretary of State's office show Sunsphere was incorporated by Robert A. Finley, a lawyer in the same firm as Howard. The address at the time of incorporation was Community Tectonics,

2206 United American Plaza, and now Plaza Tower. Finley was listed as the agent for serving legal papers on the corporation. Bob Woodson was listed as president; Rob Woodson was listed as vice-president and treasurer, and Mrs. Tackett as secretary. Board members were the Woodsons, Arnold and Sara Tackett, and Frank White, another Butcher associate.

Finley said he got involved initially because of Bill Denton. He said he didn't have anything to do with the corporation except for the legal papers.

Those who had participated in what was later described as a "hellacious" two-day session on closing the loans on the project in 1981 and Howard attended, acting on behalf of C.H. Butcher, Jr.

"My impression was that Woodson owned half of the Sunsphere and C.H. half in the name of the Tackett's," said one person who had attended that meeting.

According to Jesse Barr, Bob Woodson and Sara Tackett were fronting for C.H. in the deal.

Jesse said, "If C.H. owned part of the Sunsphere it wouldn't make any difference. It was Jake's Fair." Sandra Lea's book continues to be available for sale.

2000 Teresa's Term Paper

Teresa Miller, a student at Princeton University visited Knoxville in order to do research for a term paper she was assigned to write for one of her classes. In 2007, 29 year old Miller was a student in Stanford

University, getting a doctorate in Aeronautical Engineering.

Interview with Teresa Miller 2007:

"Why did you write about the Sunsphere?" I asked.

"I am from Oak Ridge," she said. "I took the class, CEE 262a at Princeton; because I thought it would be interesting. We were assigned a project of analyzing a building. One weekend while I was visiting home, my dad and I went over to the Sunsphere and looked around. It was closed, so we walked up the 412 steps. When we got to the top, we found that one of the doors was open on Level 4, so, we went in and looked around. Dad thought it would be a good topic for my term paper, so I went to the library and researched it. Several students in that class had written about other famous buildings, but I was the only person who researched the Sunsphere. It is an unique structure."

Miller's Term Paper in its entirety:

The Knoxville Sunsphere

Princeton University, CEE 262 a
May 9, 2000

1 Scientific

The Sunsphere in Knoxville, Tennessee was built as the theme structure for the 1982 World's Fair. The project architect was Bruce B. Thompson of Community Tectonics in Knoxville, Tennessee, and the structural engineers were Socrates A. Ioannides and Jack H. Horner of Stanley D. Lindsey and Associates of Nashville, Tennessee.

1.1 Geometry and Materials

The Knoxville Sunsphere is best described by a picture. It is a hexagonal steel truss structure 266 feet tall. The top 74 feet are shaped into a glass plate covered sphere.

The shaft of this structure consists of 6 double columns. The outer 6 columns are splayed at the bottom to provide greater stability, and end at the base of the sphere. The Interior six columns run the entire length of the structure. The two sets of columns are stiffened with k bracing

The sphere is rather unusual because the outer frame carries a significant portion of the weight. This design technique was sufficiently unusual to warrant the appearance of the Sunsphere on the front page of Engineering News Record. There are 30 curved steel columns and 13 horizontal steel hoops that form the spherical structure. These are made of 5x3 inch steel tubes. The curved steel columns are joined to the main shaft by a tension ring at the top of the sphere, and a compression ring at the bottom. These rings are 'space frames" which are constructed of various sizes of tubes (6x6 inch to 14x14 inch), selected for their good torsional characteristics. On the interior of the sphere, beams extend from the core shaft to support the weight of the observation and restaurant decks. The visual aspects of the construction process were tracked quite carefully by the local newspapers. Some of these pictures appear in Figures 4 and 5. *

The foundation of the Sunsphere consists of spread footings. This is rather unusual for the Knoxville area, as the ground is primarily limestone, which has a tendency to shift and settle. Therefore, most heavy buildings in the area are, "founded on caissons or piles to solid rock". The engineers of the Sunsphere believed that it was stable enough to not need these precautions, and thereby saved between $80,000 and $100,000.

A simple analysis of this structure is possible by looking at the effects of dead loads, live loads, and wind loads on the structure.

1.2 Dead Loads

A close inspection of the dead loads acting on the Sunsphere proved difficult, as the architects of the project no longer have these records, and it was never reported in any of the documents examined. The dead loads are therefore calculated using several approximations.

The glass walls of the sphere are estimated first. The surface area of the sphere that is Covered in glass is 16,295 ft. squared. A structural study of the John Hancock Tower estimates the weight of partitioning, exterior walls, and permanent equipment as 60 psf. {4} Using these values, the weight of the glass walls of the Sunsphere and other miscellaneous parts can be estimated as 980 kips.

The weight of concrete floors in the structure must also be considered. These can be estimated by assuming that the floors are 8 inches thick, and then, using a standard density of concrete of 150 lbs/ft cubed. This results in a weight of 100 psf. For concrete floors. The area of the floors and resulting dead and live loads are estimated in the following table. Note that the first floor is not included because it rests on the ground. It is therefore not supported by the steel structure.

The remainder of the structure is estimated by first assuming that all remaining members are the standard steel shape @ 14x61. These beams are 14 inches long between flanges, and weight 61 pounds per foot. Estimates for total feet of steel are estimated from the schematic drawing (Figure 6). ** The detailed estimate is as fol

6 interior columns	1595'	
6 interior columns	1200'	
23 floors of interior elevator bracing		2944'
5 floors of glass bracing		
2040'		
18 floors of interior K bracing		
2592'		
18 floors of exterior column bracing	1722'	
Total	12,094'	

This results in 740 kips of steel structure, and a total of 4610 kips of dead load.

1.3 Live Loads

The live loads in the structure consist primarily of visitors to the restaurant and observation decks. For an estimate of this value we may use a standard load for office buildings of 50 psf. Indeed, as the Sunsphere is currently used as an office building, this would seem to be appropriate. The square footage of the occupiable space is estimated from the schematic drawing. * Each of the top five floors on the interior of the sphere is considered occupiable, as are the bottom two levels of the tower. Again, the first floor is not considered because it is not supported by the steel structure. A summary of results appears in the table in Section 1.2.

The final estimate is 1445 kips of live load. This estimate is a generous one since the interior of the building is largely occupied by the elevator shafts and stairways. However, it is better to overestimate than underestimate.

1.4 Wind Loads

The wind loads on the structure are not expected to be very high for this structure. Because it is located in a valley it is sheltered from the worst of the wind. On one windy day after the World's Fair had ended, six passengers were caught in an elevator inside the Sunsphere when it jammed due to deflection of the tower in gusting winds. The airport approximately 10 miles away recorded gusts of 40 mph. Since the tower reacted so poorly to such light loading, it will be assumed here that the designed wind load was only 80 mph.

The unusual shape of the Sunsphere makes it subject not only to normal wind forces, but also to aerodynamic forces. The equation for aerodynamic force (drag) on a sphere is:

$$D = 1/2 \, pV^2 C_d A$$

Where p is atmospheric density, V is wind velocity, Cd is the drag coefficient of a sphere, and A is the projected area of the sphere that is exposed to the wind. Assuming atmospheric conditions and a Cd of 0.14, the force acting on the sphere is only 9.8 kips. Because this shape is relatively streamlined, the forces on it are quite small. Doing a similar analysis for the shaft of the structure and assuming an appropriate Cd of 1.2, the forces acting on the shaft are 146.2 kips. This total is 156 kips, or this comes out to .59 kips/ft., only a quarter of the estimate used for the Eiffel Tower in structural studies. However, the Sunsphere is located in a much more sheltered area, and as evidenced by the hammed elevator, was probably not designed for a very high wind load.

1.5 Efficiency

Before evaluating the efficiency of the structure, it is first necessary to determine weather wind loading should be an important consideration in the analysis. If the following equation is true, then wind loads are not generally considered significant to the design.

$$\frac{New + N\,g}{N\,9} = 4/3$$

N 9 is stress caused by wind loads and N g is stress caused by gravity loads. Assuming that the majority of the wind loads would be taken by the outer columns while the gravity loads would be divided evenly among all 12 columns, the left side of the equation yields only 1.05.

Knowing that wind loads may be neglected, the efficiency of the structure may now be calculated from the equation:

$$n = fact\ fall$$

Where fact is the actual stress and fall is the allowable stress. The actual stress is calculated by dividing the gravity loads by the area of steel bearing these loads. A
W 14 x 61 shape has a cross sectional area of 17.9 in squared. Using this knowledge and fact that there is 12 load bearing columns, the actual stress is found to be 9.40 ksi. Assuming as allowable stress of 20 ksi for steel, the Sunsphere is found to have an efficiency of 47%.

The Sunsphere was designed as the necessary "theme structure" for the 1982 World's Fair. The Sunsphere was to be Knoxville's Eiffel Tower, or Space Needle. Because the theme of the 1982 fair was to be "Energy Turns the World", the Theme Structure for the fair was to be a "Monument to the Sun, the source of all energy." The architecture firm chosen for the design was Community Tectonics. The president of this company at the time was William Denton and the founder was Hubert Bebb, a man who had experience designing structures for several World's Fairs. The original design for the Sunsphere was to be a large glass sphere on a concrete platform. The sphere would be about a hundred feet off the ground, have gold tinted windows, and would have a diameter of 86.5 feet to symbolize the 865,000 mile diameter of the sun. This idea had several problems, however. The first was that because the structure was to be built in a valley, the structure would be partially hidden by surrounding buildings and would therefore not have a very dramatic bearing over the fair site. Also, the estimated cost of this design was too high to be allowable. The architecture firm knew that it could reduce the price while raising the height if the pedestal for the sphere cold be made of steel alone.

However, Knoxville building codes forbade construction in steel for the purpose of reducing fire hazards. The World's Fair Committee appealed to the city council to make an exception to this rule and the city ruled in their favor.

The second design of the Sunsphere consisted of a 192-foot steel truss-work tower with a 74-foot diameter gold-tinted globe on top. This design was purposely made small compared to other World's Fair theme structure predecessors. Not only was it more economical, but it also addressed a concern of visitors of World's Fairs such as those in Seattle and San Antonio. At these sites the theme structures were so tall that it was difficult to see the actual fair site from inside the structure. The final construction cost of the structure was $4 million dollars. Construction was begun by Rentenbach Engineering Corporation on January 23, 1981, and the topping off ceremonies were conducted August 24, 1981. When it was completed, the Sunsphere became the first spherical building in the United States. The exterior of the sphere was constructed of 360 windows coated with 24 carat gold dust. This gives the Sunsphere its reflective golden color and while still allowing visitors to see out the windows. Furthermore, the windows conserve energy by reducing air conditioning costs for the interior. Unfortunately, each of these windows cost $1,000. The observation decks and restaurant on the interior of the sphere could be reached via three glass elevators. The observation decks were located at the top and bottom floors to provide excellent views of both the fair site and the surrounding Knoxville and Smoky Mountain areas. The second and third floors contained a restaurant with seats for 260 diners, and the fourth floor contained the kitchen for the restaurant and a VIP dining room with seats for 38 diners. A fast food concession stand was operated at the base of the Sunsphere for the duration of the World's Fair. During the World's Fair the Sunsphere was very popular. It saw an average of 60,000 visitors a day from May 1 through October 31, 1982. Visitors were charged two dollars to ride to the observation decks, and it was believed that these charges would eventually pay for the structure. The Sunsphere was owned privately, and its owners estimated that 80% of the construction costs would be recovered in the first five years, and the remaining costs would be accounted for over the next 30 years. Unfortunately, after the fair ended the Sunsphere ceased to be a popular place for visitors. The restaurant in the sphere was forced to close in March of 1984 because it was losing tremendous amounts of money. Without any income being produced by the Sunsphere, the private owners were unable to pay their loans and when the bank threatened to foreclose in 1986, the Sunsphere and its surrounding land was appraised at only $800,000. Through a long series of financial crises and several possession transfers, the Sunsphere eventually came to be owned by the city. The Sunsphere has also been used as housing for construction workers doing renovations on the structure, a reception hall for weddings, and most recently, the offices of the Knoxville Convention and Tourist Bureau.

To better understand the costs involved in this structure, it is useful to make a comparison to a similar structure, the Seattle Space Needle. The Space Needle was built for the 1962 World's Fair. It is a total of 604 feet tall and has a maximum diameter at the top of 138 feet. The top of the Space Needle contains stores, revolving restaurants, a lounge, and an outdoor observation deck. The Space Needle is also a steel structure, and it cost 4.5 million dollars to construct. To compare this to the Knoxville Sunsphere, the scale is first adjusted. Scaling by height, the Space Needle would have cost 1.98 million dollars if it were the height of the Sunsphere. However, it was constructed in 1961 instead of 1981. Adjusting for this, the price of the Space Needle would be 8.26 million dollars. Compared to the 4 million dollar price of the Sunsphere, the Space Needle seems very expensive.

However, the comparison is not completely fair. The Space Needle continues to be a popular place to visit and dine, and therefore continues to provide revenue to its owners. It has been voted by local magazines and newspapers to be the most romantic place to dine or to propose marriage in the Northwest. One of its two restaurants has been chosen as one of the top 25 independent restaurants in the country.

In comparison, the Knoxville Sunsphere's restaurant got very poor reviews during the World's Fair, closed in 1984, and no restaurant or other industry has been willing to occupy the space. Some critics have suggested that the reason is because the interior of the Sunsphere offers so little space. The Space Needle has approximately 10,000 feet squared of restaurant space, whereas the Sunsphere only has 6,000 feet squared. If a restaurant were to be successful it would have no room to spread out. Also, in 1986 the Sunsphere cost $3 per square foot per day just to pay utilities. This would seem to suggest that the increased price of the Space Needle was justified because the added space allowed more flexibility in its use.

3.Symbolic

As the Sunsphere was originally built it was a beautiful and appropriate structure to serve as a monument to the sun. The base is splayed and the structure is hexagonal in shape to give a strong appearance of stability. Originally there were three glass elevators on the interior of the structure. This design left a great deal of open space in the pedestal, so the truss appeared to be very light when viewed from the exterior. Furthermore, the space underneath the pedestal was left open except for a single concession stand. This open space helped to provide a part-like atmosphere that was congruent with the carefully planned fair grounds surrounding the structure.

The sphere itself is quite lovely from the exterior. When it is hit by the sun it sparkles brightly and provides a beautiful and appropriate monument to the sun. The lower observation deck on the interior of the sphere is not large but provides an excellent view of the fair grounds. The higher levels where the restaurant was located during the fair was reported by visitors to be an enchanting place to dine in spite of the fact that the food was overpriced and not especially tasty.

The only possible criticism of the structure as it was originally constructed might be that it is not as prominent a structure in the city as it should have been. It was built in a valley very close to an elevated bridge that splits the fairgrounds. These two features often make the structure very difficult to see. There are many parts of downtown Knoxville from which it is impossible to see the Sunsphere because it is behind a hill. In contrast, it is possible to see the Seattle Space Needle from almost any point in the city. Also, when a visitor to the fairgrounds looks at the structure the chances are that the bottom portion will be obscured by the bridge, making it appear even shorter than it is. To make the most advantage of this structure it should have been built at least partway up a hill without any other structures immediately obscuring the view.

In spite of the difficulty seeing this structure at times, it is still a very important feature of the Knoxville area. Because of its unusual shape, the Sunsphere is immediately recognizable in a drawing of the skyline.

Without this structure in the city, Knoxville would have a completely unrecognizable profile. Furthermore, the existence of the Sunsphere is often the only thing people know about Knoxville. In older generations this is because of memories of the prominence of the structure in the 1982 World's Fair. In younger generations it seems too often to be because they have watched the Simpson's television show in which Bart visits Knoxville and accidentally knocks over the Sunsphere.

Recent changes to the Sunsphere have, unfortunately, not been beneficial to the appearance of the structure. The original design of the pedestal left the glass elevators open to the elements where they corroded. When the Convention and Tourist Bureau moved into the structure they did a great deal of remodeling. This included filling in the structure underneath the pedestal with a reception area. Also, the elevator shafts were enclosed by a material that appears to be vinyl siding. Shrouding the area of the elevators shafts, however necessary, reduces the light appearance of the structure. Also, the construction underneath the pedestal eliminates the park-like atmosphere that formerly existed. Furthermore, since the end of the World's Fair, the grounds of the site have gradually deteriorated to the point where they now appear to be little more than a burial ground for disintegrating concrete.

Without the lovely grounds underneath or the pleasure the glass elevator ride, the cramped observation deck might make a visitor wonder if this structure was really worth what it cost to build. To be fair, the observation deck is not open to the public and the pictures that appear in this paper are the result of the photographer sneaking into the structure. It is obvious from the interior, however, why the deck is not open. The windows don't appear to have been cleaned in many years and so all of Knoxville looks as if it was covered in a thick coat of smog. The displays around the deck pointing out the sights of Knoxville are no less than 10 years old, and the carpeting is probably the original. On the whole, the structure would appear to be appropriate for the signature piece of what the Wall Street Journal called a "scruffy little city."

It is expected that the upcoming modifications to the area will be an improvement. The nearby Knoxville Convention Center is constructing a second building on a corner of the fair grounds and is demolishing several of the older buildings on the site. After this is completed the Center plans to do extensive landscaping of the fair grounds to restore some of the former beauty to the area. Local newspapers report, as they have since 1984, that several restaurant owners are considering leasing several floors on the interior of the Sunsphere. Considering the additional people the Convention Center will attract, a restaurant could be a successful venture.

Regardless of the details of the appearance of the structure, Knoxville residents are likely to continue taking pride in the Sunsphere for its past and the recognition it brings to the city. The World's Fair site continues to be a centerpiece of Knoxville because of the concerts held in the outdoor amphitheater during the summer, the Fourth of July and Labor Day celebrations, and the many summer festivals held on the grounds. The structure has been beneficial to the city and, hopefully, will continue to beautify the area.

~It is this fact that led the city to put the Tourist's Bureau in the top of the sphere.

Letter from Teresa Miller June 25, 2007

Dear Ms. Woodward,

It was great talking to you on the phone the other day! I just wanted to send this letter to confirm that you may use the term paper on the Sunsphere however you like in the book you're writing. Good luck with that! You said you also wanted a little biography so here goes—feel free to edit it!

I graduated Oak Ridge High School in 1995 and went on to Princeton University where I wrote the term paper on the Sunsphere in Civil Engineering class "Structures and the Urban Environment". I graduated Princeton in 200 with a degree in Mechanical and Aerospace Engineering, and then went on to Stanford University where I got a Master's Degree and am currently working on my Ph. D. in Aeronautical and Astronautical Engineering. My thesis work has been in control of a rock climbing robot. I expect to graduate in summer of 2007 and then work in the field of medical robots. In my free time I enjoy knitting, reading, skiing, and biking and traveling to visit my family.

Again, best of luck with your book!

Sincerely,

Teresa Miller

*** Teresa Miller's paper is reprinted with her permission and with attribution to her sources as well. Not all photos are shown due to copyright rules.

2000

Climb the Tower; Stop the Bombs

   Protestors from a group known as Earth First, who are against using nuclear weapons have often been seen around Knoxville and Oak Ridge. The Knoxville community awoke one morning to the news that a two of these protestors had climbed the tower of the Sunsphere during the night and had hung a huge sign, Stop the Bombs. Chris Irwin and Duane Kuppinger not only hung the sign, they also tied cots in place and declared that they were staying as long as needed to make their point.

   When the sign was spotted, calls came in to the police department and an officer was dispatched to the scene. The protesters were approached by Knoxville Police officers and asked to climb down, and remove the sign. The protesters refused to climb back down, and remained on the tower for three days.

   This was purely a publicity stunt and was handled by the City Police Department in such a way as to have a peaceful resolution.

   Foster Arnett, who was the spokesperson for the Knoxville Police Department at the time, said that the decision was made to wait them out. "We could deploy our special operations squad and bring them down, but that could end up with someone getting hurt," Mr. Arnett said. The men were charged with trespassing after they came down from the tower and no one was harmed. (Knoxville News-Sentinel, 5-16-00, Jennifer Johnson)

2000   Rented as office space

   The Public Building Authority kept offices on the 7th floor in the Sunsphere while the new convention center was being built.

   Denark-Smith of Knoxville and Clark Construction of Tampa, Florida, contractors for the convention center and related improvements to the park grounds, as well as their subcontractors, used office space on levels 6 and 8.

   It is estimated that approximately 50 people used the building during those years. (Balloch, Jim, 11-5-99)

2000 until 2007

        Park Patrol

   More uses:

   Bill Plankers of the Park Patrol reports that the Park Patrol kept offices in the Sunsphere for several years, but moved out when their new office building was built on the World's Fair Park site.

   "It is not the kind of building that is good space for the kind of work we do," he said. "We are out in the park all day, and it could be time consuming to need something that was up on the 8th floor of the Sunsphere. We do much better from the new offices."

2002 Bayterek-Astana, Kazakhstan

Doing research is a lot like mining for gold. You have to sift through a lot of useless material to find one nugget that is worthwhile. As I did research about the Knoxville Sunsphere, I found out about another spherical tower which was built in 2002 in Kazakhstan. Yes, Kazakhstan is the country which has been made famous by the Borat movie.

For most years of its life, the Sunsphere in Knoxville has been known as the only spherical tower in the world. That is no longer true. A 386 ft. tower has been built in Astana, Kazakhstan which is named Bayterek. It looks remarkably like the Sunsphere in Knoxville, Tennessee. Bayterek is 96 meters tall with the sphere being 22 meters high. That converts to about 314 feet tall and 72 feet for the sphere, making the tower taller than our Sunsphere, with the sphere being somewhat smaller.

The sources who describe the Bayterek tower say that there is a legend of a magical bird, named Samruk, who laid an egg in a tall poplar tree. The tower is located in the new capital city of Astana, Kazakhstan.

According to an article on wikipedia.org, Bayterek, from the Kazakh for "tall poplar tree" is a new monument in Astana, the capital of Kazakhstan. Bayterek has become a popular tourist attraction with visitors and native Kazakhstanis alike, symbolizing the new status of the young capital of Kazakhstan, Astana. The top of the complex structure is a gilt sphere crowning a mythological tree of 97 meters. (314 ft.)

The monument is lighted at night, and appears in bank notes, advertisements, and all kinds of printed material, similar to the way the Knoxville Sunsphere has been used throughout the years, although the Sunsphere has never been used on printed money.

While writing this book, I have refrained from giving my personal opinions, however, it is obvious that this tower was modeled after the Knoxville Sunsphere. The golden ball with the levels of floors on the inside, and the idea of a tower that was built as a theme structure for the new city, are too similar to the Sunsphere in Knoxville to have been a mere coincidence. I have heard that imitation is a form of flattery. I suppose the builders of the Knoxville Sunsphere can feel pride when they see Bayterek, since it appears to be a copy of their ideas and designs. (Wikipedia, Bayterek)

Photo of Bayterek, a building designed from the plans of the Sunsphere.

2002 Give me Twenty

1982 World's Fair served as catalyst to unify community

By Randy Tyree, Guest columnist
August 11, 2002

Knoxville News-Sentinel

The articles commemorating Knoxville's 1982 World's Fair were excellent, both in quality and quantity. They sparked wonderful memories of a time when our community grabbed hold of Andy Warhol's fifteen minutes of fame and transformed them into 180 days of activity that was exciting, educational, entertaining and forever memorable.

Your editorial reference to our community working hard and successfully achieving a broad base of minority involvement in the fair was especially gratifying. There were limited economic opportunities and limited leadership roles for African Americans and women existing in Knoxville in the '70s and early '80s, and the fair provided numerous opportunities to address those limitations. It did so effectively.

An initial leadership role for the African-American community was provided by former City Council member Theotis Robinson, who was the fourth staff person hired by the fair and served as vice president of economic development. Under his direction, a formula was established which targeted a 12 percent to 18 percent minority participation in the fair.

Such participation wasn't required by law; it was done because it was the right thing to do and made economic sense since more than 18 million black consumers - 72 percent of the nation's population - live within a day's drive of Knoxville. Additionally, 12 percent of the concession stands were minority owned, and the pavilions of Japan, Mexico and the Philippines were engineered and constructed by African-American firms.

There were scores of other jobs created, which ran the gamut from VIP hostesses and security guards to the more traditional office and maintenance workers. Significant minority participation occurred in all three phases of the fair, from the planning and development through close down.

Reprinted by permission of the writer.

2003 The birds The birds The birds

Anyone who has spent very much time around the Sunsphere will readily tell you that the birds, mainly, pigeons and starlings, are one of the major problems the Public Building Authority faces in maintaining the structure. This problem did not begin in 2003; it has been an on-going issue since 1982.

Pigeons-pipionis, and starlings- Sturnidae, fly onto the tower, and many of them nest there. All of them poop there, and it is the poop that is an expensive reminder of their visits. It has been estimated that over 300 birds per hour stop for a visit at the Sunsphere during Spring and Summer, and again in the late Fall. Park employees report that there are times when it seems like a scene from Alfred Hitchcock's movie "The Birds." Witnesses report seeing thousands of the small birds flying onto the Sunsphere, loudly chirping and flapping their wings.

The poop is a problem because the uric acid found in the droppings is toxic. The birds also build nests and hatch young from crevices in the tower. Caretakers of the Sunsphere are not always certain how the birds find their way into the insides of the tower. It is not unusual for live birds to be found flying around inside all levels of the sphere. Over the years, hundreds of birds' nests have been removed from the Sunsphere. Not only have nests been removed, but eggs, dead birds, feathers, sticks, parts of paper, and various other things which have been carried 266 feet into the air by the 9 inch, 3 ounce menaces.

The City Officials have used various methods in dealing with the problems of the birds. One such method involved the use of a tape recording of animal sounds which was played in hopes of chasing the birds away. This method was met with outcries from the people who live in the neighborhood and was, eventually, stopped.

"I was about to cook some dinner when I got home from work one afternoon," stated a student who lived in an apartment complex near the Sunsphere. All of the sudden I heard what sounded like a lion or tiger growling. Next came the screeching of eagles, and the barking of dogs. I ran outside to see what was happening, but didn't see anything. Some other people were outside, and we stood and discussed the sounds. Some thought they could hear pigs squealing, Several people phoned 9ll and a policeman came. He told us that the City was trying to get rid of the birds. We didn't care, but, they could have sent us a letter or something. It was kind of scary. We went back to our apartments, and read about it the paper a few days later."

The city abandoned the idea of using animal sounds saying it did not work.

Birds see the Sunsphere as a place to roost and to nest. Its height makes it attractive, as well, because it appears to simply be a very large tree to a bird. We may not see the Sunsphere as a source of food, but the birds do. So long as there is food being carried into the tower, it will be a magnet for birds.

Dealing with the birds and cleaning up bird poop remain on-going problems. Work crews are attempting to seal up the elevators, hoping that this keeps the birds from getting inside the 5 levels in the golden ball, and loud speakers have been installed which can be used as a way of playing sounds or music to discourage the birds from taking up residency in the tower.

Other animals who love the Sunsphere are wasps and bees. Park patrol officers say that they are constantly removing nests as well as watching for angry insects.

"We make an effort to look for them before they can take hold," said one officer. "No one wants to deal with a huge nest of angry insects. We do not know why they love the Sunsphere, maybe it is the way the light gets reflected off of it, but insects do love it."

(Higgins, Trevor, 12-30-03)

2004

New Mayor; same problems

As Bill Haslam assumed the office of mayor in January of 2004, the Sunsphere sat empty, except for a few people who worked for the Park Patrol who checked on it every day. It was, mainly, used by the birds. Mayor Haslam promised to fix the problems associated with the Sunsphere and make it useful and profitable. The mayor called for input from the community. Tours were conducted and various people and groups were invited to attend these tours and to give their ideas. As it seems to go with Mayor Haslam, after listening to all the ideas from a varied group of individuals, he decided to make a deal with his friends of Kinsey-Probasco-Hays of Chattanooga who are connected to Senator Bob Corker. It is not known why the mayor did not choose a local firm to do the work. Also, Mayor Haslam negotiated a deal with Southern Graces, a catering firm, who will pay a lease of $70,000 per year in order to place a snack bar, wet bar, and use levels 5 and 6 as rental space for events and a catering business. The yearly electrical bill for the Sunsphere is said to be approximately $45,000 to $50,000; some estimates have it nearer to $95,000 per year.

"It is difficult to answer people who ask why they can't get into the Sunsphere," said Mayor Haslam when he came to office. (Trenda, Hilary, 9-7-06)

(Many local folks believe that John Kinsey and Brian Conley have saved the Sunsphere by agreeing to this lease).

2007

Knoxville's Arts and Culture Alliance

The agency known as the Arts Council went out of business in 2002. Another similar agency, which broadened the scope of the goals of the former Arts Council, was formed and is known as Knoxville's Arts & Culture Alliance. This group is not a part of the city government, but the city's web page contains a lengthy reference to the numerous events which are sponsored by it.

The Alliance is a 501 3 C non-profit agency which exists to promote painting, sculpture, photography, ballet, opera, theatre, travel, pottery, live performances, movies, music, history, and much, much more. Their offices are located in the Emporium Building which houses the Rodman Townsend, Sr. Memorial Gallery 100 S.Gay Street. They have several employees, who are paid from donations and dues, as well as from fund-raising events. Also, as a non-profit 5013C organization, they have hundreds of volunteers who give time to the community in numerous worthwhile projects. They continue to show interest in the Sunsphere.

May 2007   All debts for World's Fair paid

A press release was sent out in May of 2007 saying that the city of Knoxville had paid all debts which had been taken out 25 years ago to finance the World's Fairs. Randy Kenner, who was hired in 2006 by Mayor Bill Haslam as Communications Coordinator for the city of Knoxville, announced that the city had made the final payment on $46 million dollars in bonds which were taken out to pay for the World's Fair. At one point, it was thought that it would take until 2009 to get this debt paid, but the city was able to pay it by June 1, 2007. (internet press release 5-07; Kenner)

July 3, 2007
   Mayor Haslam announces Level 4 of the Sunsphere is opened to the public.
   In a press release that was sent to me by e-mail, Mayor Haslam's office announced a "ribbon-cutting" on the reopening of the Sunsphere. (Kenner, Randy, 7-3-07)

July 4, 2007
   Dane Bradshaw, former University of Tennessee basketball star, rode a zip line from the top of the
Sunsphere to the yard in the World's Fair Park to celebrate the day.

July 5, 2007   Opened to the public
   After being closed since 1999, the Sunsphere opened to the public with the announcement that visitors could travel up the elevators to Level 4 (or the first level in the golden ball).By noon on July 5th, a steady stream of visitors were arriving at the Sunsphere; many from as far away as Tampa, Florida. Young mothers with children, grandmothers with their grandchildren, photographers, businessmen, couples, and media types were touring the newly opened landmark. The Park Patrol said that approximately 60 people per hour were visiting the newly opened icon. The windows had been washed and painted. A handrail had been installed encircling the entire floor. Exhibits and displays that give the essence of the World's
Fair were tastefully displayed. A flat screen television played vintage videos from the opening and closing ceremonies of the Fair, along with other videos of parades, musical performances, and speeches from the six months in which the Fair was in operation.

December 2007
   Sukenik of Southern Graces Catering and Event Planning Says He's Having a Big Year
After months of wrangling with fire codes, electrical problems, bird poop, tearing down walls, antiquated equipment and just about everything else, in December 2009, Robert Sukenik told reporter, Carly Harrington, of the Knoxville News Sentinel, "This has been a difficult experience getting this thing the right way because it is a 25 year structure like no other." Sukenik rented the 5th and 6th floors of the building for approximately $10,500 a month plus some percentage of the utilities. He chose to remodel the 5th floor and, eventually, used more than $100,000 to $200,000 of his own money to make the needed repairs. Some say his choices of high end décor' were over the top and ran the costs up too high. 2009 was a banner year for Sukenik as he had over 200 events booked for the year. However, although many of his customers were pleased with the way their events turned out, others were not and repeat customers did not happen for the optimistic businessman. Rumors of debt, employees being asked to wait for paychecks, lack-luster service, and small servings of tasteless food could not be overcome. "It is one thing to ask people to pay $3,000 to book your site," said one customer who would prefer to go unnamed, "it's quite another to serve yucky food that no one would eat. I was embarrassed for myself, Sukenik, the Sunsphere and my guests. One of my guests said the chicken looked like cat food. No one liked the hard crackers either."

September 2009

After working for Bob Sukenik and Southern Graces and seeing the Sunsphere go through many changes, and after Sukenik went down in flames for the last time, Sara Spangler decided to negotiate a deal with Kinsey-Probosco and Hays and hire on as the booking agent for the 6th floor of the Sunsphere. Spangler explains how the deal works in the following posts.

The 6th floor is, generally, where most social and business events are held in that building. Since that time until present (May 2014), Spangler has been able to keep the building busy.

From Sara Spangler--Prolific Living, LLC. --Booking Agent for the Sunsphere

The Sunsphere building is owned by the City of Knoxville. The iconic landmark features a Public observation deck on Floor 4, and a large Event Venue on Floor 6. Private businesses occupy floors 5, 7, and 8 - including the administrative offices of Cardinal Enterprises, Apollo Asset Management, and Prolific Living.

The 266-foot tall structure was renovated in 2007 and is leased from the City by the developers of the renovation project; Kinsey Probasco Hays of Chattanooga and Knoxville based Cardinal Enterprises. The Developers hold a 20-year lease on the Sunsphere building. Apollo Asset Management (a division of Cardinal Enterprises) manages floors 5-8 of the property and also controls the lease agreements on the Event Floor. In late 2010 Apollo Asset Management entered into an agreement with small Event, Media, and Public Relations firm Prolific Living to exclusively book the Event Floor.

Prolific Living serves as the liaison between any Sunsphere Event Floor client and Apollo Asset Management. The Firm coordinates referrals and communications between clients and vendors associated with any party held on the Event Floor and maintains excellent relationships with Knoxville's most trusted event professionals. While some of these companies are listed on our Partner Page, we welcome the opportunity to work with any proven event professional of our client's choice. Prolific Living was chosen to represent the Sunsphere icon to offer Event Floor clients the benefit of their vast experience and knowledge of private events in the Knoxville area -as well as in larger markets such as Nashville and Los Angeles. The relationship offers a sense of security for the Event Floor client due to the contracts being held by a long- term landlord. (Apollo Asset Management) The affiliation between Apollo Asset Management and Prolific Living is a perfect balance of solid contractual implementation and savvy event direction and execution.

The Sunsphere Event Floor is proud to work closely with The Public Building Authority to double our efforts in promoting the historic park for your next event. Weddings at the Amphitheater (the only other surviving structure from the 1982 World's Fair) coupled with a reception on the Sunsphere Event Floor have become a very popular option for Knoxville brides. In addition, large festivals and fundraising events on the World's Fair Park Lawn can rent the Sunsphere Event Floor - a VIP kick-off or wrap party over- looking the park is an impressive extra for festival vendors and contributors! The Observation Deck (housed on Floor 4) is managed by Public Building Authority, as are any other rental areas on the World's Fair Park grounds. For any questions pertaining to the Public Observation deck or other World's Fair Park properties, please visit worldsfairpark.org or call Dorissa Simpson at 865.251.6861

The Sunsphere Event Floor
The 6th floor of the Sunsphere is the largest floor of the structure, and is the only floor available for event rentals. The Event Floor boasts a 360-degree view of Knoxville with floor to ceiling windows. Nicknamed by many guests as "The Social Venue – the Sunsphere Event Floor's design encourages conversation and movement. Everyone has experienced an event where one group stayed on one side of the room and another group "cliqued' off to the opposite side. The circular layout affords our guests the opportunity to enjoy the entire room and socialize with more of the crowd. Promoting conversation amongst your guests are the different landmarks in Knoxville to experience on each side: North, South, East and West. We offer a variety of specialty room set-ups and have a generous amount of food and bar service tables ready for use.

The Sunsphere Event Floor also offers a fantastic audio -visual system with surround sound and 3 HD Plasma flat-screened televisions tastefully mounted in focal points of the room. Weddings have become popular on the event floor as the room can easily be "flipped" from rowed seating/ceremony to reception set up. From corporate power lunches and promotional dinners to intimate weddings, the Sunsphere has hosted a variety of events since re-opening in November 2010. Our grand re-opening in March in conjunction with First Friday hosted over 600 people over the course of the evening and afforded the general public the opportunity to experience a party at the top! We are proud to be able to offer our clients numerous choices for having a custom party to fit their needs. We allow any caterer of choice to service events and can refer various bar service options.

Rentals are for three hours - additional time can be added at $350 per hour. Adequate set up and break down time is provided for every event. We have the following tables/chairs that come with the venue rental:

- (150) Chiavari Mahogany Chairs with black chair cushions
- (15) 60' round guest tables (can seat 8-10 people per table)
- (2) 6 foot rectangular tables
- (2) 8 foot rectangular tables
- (1) 48' round cake table
- (3) Glass and wood high top cocktail tables
- Complete audio/visual system, i-Pod docking station, and 3 flat screen plasma TV's &surround sound throughout event floor

Every event rental is different; pricing will be in line with venue demand and size of party. For the quickest rental quote and venue availability, please e-mail your request to sara@sunsphereeventrentals or call direct to 865.363.9538 Phone calls received by 4pm on a business day will be returned as quickly as possible, however e-mail quotes can usually be delivered within minutes of a request and also on weekends.

Sara Spangler at the Sunsphere.

Tony Cappiello's Ultra Iconic Lounge 2011

By the time the month of June rolled around in 2011, Tony Cappiello, a developer from Oak Ridge, began to discuss his plans for an upscale night club he was hoping to open on the fifth floor of the Sunsphere.

Developer Tony Cappiello leased the space, formerly named Skybox. Skybox had been a bar created by Bob Sukenik of Southern Graces. Skybox remained in business for three years, but closed with Sukenik was forced out of the building due to overspending on remodeling and a flawed business plan for event planning.

Cappiello was already referring to his new venture as an "Ultra Lounge," which he said would be similar to what one might see in Las Vegas, New Orleans, or Los Angeles.

When interviewed by Stony Sharp of WBIR-TV, Cappiello presented his ideas for a "Sun Bar" and a "Rain Bar," both of which would be positioned on the 5th floor in order to take advantage of the rising and setting of the sun.

Cappiello was targeting a late September 2011 or early October opening, however, this date was pushed forward by over a year due to the demands of the Public Building Authority and City Codes Department.

Meanwhile, the sixth floor continued to be an event venue rented through Sara Spangler, who has exclusive booking rights to the space. She began renting the floor in December 2010 with a deal made with Chad Copenhauer, who held the lease for that floor.

Icon Ultra Lounge on the fifth floor of the Sunsphere

Posted by **The Knoxville Journal** on November 15th, 2012

After months of struggling with fire codes and regulations from the Public Building Authority, Tony Cappiello has opened the Icon Ultra Lounge on the fifth floor of the Sunsphere. Cappiello, who has exclusive rental rights to the space on the fifth floor of the 30-year-old theme structure of the 1982 World's Fair, said he has invested an estimated $450,000 to renovate the space. The capacity is now 120 making it three times larger than its predecessor, The Skybox. Cappiello said he chose to light up the floors, bars and tables so guests could be "wowed by the experience".

Cappiello said his plans took into consideration the panoramic view and placed seating in special areas so guests could enjoy the sunsets. He added two-seat tables near the windows and large, over-stuffed booths to round out the new theme.

A new electrical system was installed, the floor was reworked and stained sky blue and a fireplace was added to create a cozy corner. A DJ booth, a second bar and two additional restrooms were also added.

The Rain Bar, which has a continuous stream of water that flows through the bar top and into a nearby water wall, is on one side. The Sun Bar is on the other side and is topped with onyx and covered with gold tufted panels aimed at capturing the look of the famous gold glass panels.

Cappiello said he studied other bars in cities such as Chicago, Las Vegas and New Orleans. "We wanted to make it an upscale, higher-end establishment," he said.

Cappiello is an attorney and developer who also purchased the Lord Lindsey, another downtown landmark that he plans to convert into a nightclub. Cappiello said he enjoyed designing the Icon Ultra Lounge himself. "Choosing the colors, materials and furniture is one of my favorite parts in the process," he said.

Since parking is always a problem at the Sunsphere, Cappiello said spaces are available at the nearby Knoxville Museum of Art, in the lot next to Church Street United Methodist Church and the Locust Street parking garage next to the YMCA. He says he will provide a golf cart to circle the grounds and plans to add a valet service in the future.

Icon Ultra Lounge is closed on Mondays and is open 4 p.m. to midnight Tuesdays and Wednesdays and 4 p.m. to 3 a.m. Thursdays through Saturdays.

The fourth floor of the Sunsphere contains the Observation Center and is open from dawn to dusk most days of the year. It is free to the public, however, shoes and shirt are required. Children must be accompanied by an adult. No swimwear allowed. The sixth floor of the Sunsphere is open for rental through Sara Spangler and can be used for small to large parties, weddings, and other events. *By Martha Woodward*

**The 7th Floor contains office space for
Cardinal Enterprises.**

A beautiful day at the Sunsphere.

Events take place at lunch as well as
breakfast and dinner on the 6th floor of the
Sunsphere

WBIR-TV Stoney Sharp and photographer
doing a story around Halloween 2013 on 4th
floor of the Sunsphere.

Frequently asked questions:

Does the Sunsphere revolve?

No, it has never revolved. The restaurant on the Space Needle, which is located in Seattle, Washington, does revolve. People often get the two structures confused. The Space Needle is over 600 feet tall, while the Sunsphere is 266 feet tall, with the tower being 192, and the globe 74. Also, after the World's Fair closed in 1982, the Sunsphere Restaurant advertised a "revolving lights show" in which the Sunsphere was wired in such a way that, at night, the lights made it appear to revolve. The building itself has never revolved. There was discussion of making the Sunsphere revolve, however this would have added costs to an, already, tight budget.

What is the address of the Sunsphere? 810 Clinch Avenue, Knoxville, Tennessee 37901 is the official address.

Why do some people say there are 5 levels, and others say there are 8 levels?

The people who write about the Sunsphere often do not do their homework. The Sunsphere has 3 levels which are ground and street level, and 5 levels which are 192 feet in the air. Levels 4 to 8 are sometimes renamed as Levels 1 to 5. Please see photos of the blueprints for an explanation and diagram.

Who came up with the name Sunsphere?

William Denton, of Community Tectonics, is credited with thinking of the name for the spherical tower on a day in November, 1981.

What happened to the glass elevators?

Like all things in this world, the glass elevators simply wore out. They were replaced in 1992 and the elevator shaft was framed in with vinyl siding as a safety feature. City officials were fearful that someone might get injured on the elevators.

What would it cost to build the Sunsphere in 2011?

It has been estimated that in today's dollars, the Sunsphere would cost $50 to $60 million dollars. If built in 2007, the Sunsphere would have to conform to the Americans With Disabilities Act and other codes, which could cause the price to skyrocket.

Why has the Sunsphere been neglected?

As with most things in government, there has often been a "turf" battle concerning the Sunsphere. The Sunsphere was built during administration of a Democrat, Randy Tyree. The following Republican mayors have continued to think of the structure as something that was done by the Democrats.

Also, the workings of a government are complicated. Other issues took precedence over the needs of the Sunsphere. City officials were seeking something that would draw in tourists. The issues which have been cited as challenges or problems with the Sunsphere are: lack of adequate space, parking, location, high prices for food and beverages, the difficulties of hauling all items up and down the elevators, time required to wait for the elevators, and the inability of having space to promote growth.

Does the Sunsphere sway or move?

Yes, the building was built to "give" or sway. William Denton explained this movement to me. "It is like a floor lamp," he said, "when it is pushed on one side, it does not fall, and it sways some and settles back. This is because the weight in the base is more than the force which pushed on it; same way with the Sunsphere. When a wind gust of less than 100 mph pushes on the Sunsphere, it moves some, but, the weight of the concrete in its base, pulls it back into the erect position."

Some people say that they feel nausea or seasickness from being in the upper floors of the building when it moves.

Are there restrooms in the Sunsphere?

Yes, there are two restrooms, one for women; one for men, in levels four, five, six, seven, and eight. These restrooms are also handicapped accessible which means that the architects who built the Sunsphere were forward thinking.

How long does it take to ride up the elevators?

186 seconds from the lowest point on the ground, to the highest point in level 8 and back.

Why has the elevator shaft been covered with vinyl siding?

The elevators were sealed as a safety precaution and because of the problem caused by birds roosting on the tower. The use of vinyl siding was done because it is a building material that does not require a lot of maintenance, and the cost was what the city could afford at the time.

Why doesn't the city tear down the Sunsphere and make room for other buildings that might be more profitable?

The Sunsphere is an icon and a landmark. It is the most recognizable building in Knoxville. Citizens love the Sunsphere. Also, it would cost millions of dollars to tear it down, and haul away the steel and glass. How many steps are on the fire escape? There are 418 steps on each of two stairways, for a total of 836. How much have the Sunsphere cost the taxpayers of this city and county?

A low estimate of the cost of the Sunsphere for the last 26 years would be $12 million dollars. The cost could be more like $15 million to $20 million, however. The structure originally cost $6.6 million to build in 1981.

Many of the renovations and repair costs have been reported as a part of the overall budget of the Public Building Authority, making it almost impossible to put an exact amount on the total cost. City officials are not sure, and are evasive, at best, when this question is posed to them. Written reports which have been published in local newspapers, can be totaled, along with utility bills, repair costs, maintenance bills, as well as salaries for people who take care of the Sunsphere, and for those who guard it. $12 million is a safe guess. To put it into some kind of perspective, the Sunsphere costs each person in the city of Knoxville about $55 dollars per year, and will continue to cost that much or more well into the future.

Why do you refer to the Sunsphere as a landmark?

Historically, a landmark was any geographical feature used by explorers and others to find their way back or through an area. In modern usage, it means anything that is recognizable, such as a building, a monument, bridge, or other structure. It is also used to refer to a place that might be of interest to tourists.

Who owns the Sunsphere?

The City of Knoxville purchased it for $750,000 in 1986.

Has the Sunsphere ever produced revenue?

Yes, during the 6 months of the World's Fair, the Sunsphere made money. Also, during the years it was used by the Arts Council revenue was brought in by renting space for special events.

Has anyone ever climbed the Sunsphere?

Although it is illegal to climb the tower of the Sunsphere, some individuals have done so. This is extremely dangerous. The Park Patrol is constantly watching the Sunsphere to prevent anyone from getting hurt.

To write a book...

As you read this book, I would like for you to consider a statement about history told to me by a historian, my Daddy who passed away in 1996. I believe that he gave some good advice.

James Roy Woodward (1915-1996), my dad, along with Helen Gibbs Woodward, my mother (1921-1990), lived 51 years in Lawrence County, Tennessee in a rural hamlet called Leoma, located five miles south of Lawrenceburg on Highway 43.

Daddy made a remarkable statement to me one day when he had turned 80 years old. I happened to be visiting him in the hospital, and the television was tuned to one of those documentary programs about World War II. Since he was a veteran who landed in Normandy on the second day of the attack, he was always interested in that kind of a thing.

"That's not right, Cis," he said, and pointed to the television.

"What's wrong, Daddy?" I asked, and I could tell that he was upset.

"What those people are saying is not the way it happened. I know," he continued, "I was there."

"How was it different?" I asked.

"Lots of ways," he said. Next, Daddy said something that would be good advice for any person who sits down to write about history. It was one of those statements that tend to stick with a person. Daddy said, "History needs to be written by the people who lived it, Cis."

My Daddy was right.

I am following Daddy's advice. I am writing about something in history that I lived through. I have personal memories of most of the things in this book. Also, I have been fortunate that most of the people who were in leadership positions and actually made the decisions about the Sunsphere, graciously agreed to sit with me for interviews. To the best of my ability, everything that I have written in this book is a true account of living history.

I want the readers to know that I do not have a hidden agenda. I have not set out to get anyone. My motives come from a place of curiosity and intrigue. My goals were to write a historically correct book while also making it beautiful.

Doug Young, my good friend, during a meeting we held at the Sunsphere in 2009.

Doug passed away in 2013.

Lee Wilson's 1982 book commissioned by William Denton.

Real History:
The Sunsphere and Other Famous Structures of Past World's Fairs
   By Lee Wilson

   In 1982, Community Tectonics hired a local writer, Lee Wilson, to write a book which was sold at the World's Fair for a few dollars. Since the book is out of print, and since they hold all copyrights, I have been given permission to use excerpts and photos from it.

   The follow excerpt was actually written by William Denton and typed by Janice Sullivan and remains the most factual record of the beginnings of the Sunsphere in existence.

   This excerpt is taken from pages 31 to 70 of the informative

   book: The Sunsphere Story

Man's newest monument to the sun is an exhibition structure—the Sunsphere, the theme structure for the 1982 World's Fair. It is a beautiful mirrored golden glass globe held aloft over the Fair site by a graceful tower of blue steel and is the first permanent spherical building of any consequence on earth. The Sunsphere represents the sun, the source of all the earth's energy, and reflects the energy theme of the Fair. The Sunsphere is symbolic of the fair's purpose, the gathering together of the best energy ideas and innovations from 22 countries and many corporations to enlighten and excite and inspire those who came to the Fair to see them. Without the Sunsphere the Fair would have been like a symphony without a title, but the logistical and technical problems facing the developers of the Sunsphere very nearly decreed that it would remain forever only a set of sketches in an architect's file cabinet.

   The Sunsphere had its genesis at a meeting one November in 1979 at the Knoxville office of Community Tectonics, Inc., an East Tennessee architectural firm. The main order of business, plans for a fast food restaurant, had been disposed of when Litton Cochran, owner of the restaurant and a member of the 1982 World's Fair management committee, mentioned that the Fair as yet had no theme structure or focal point, though planning for the event was well under way. Cochran, as he had several times before, asked the Community Tectonics architects, among whom were Hubert Bebb, a founder of the firm, and Bill Denton, its president, if they would submit to the committee a proposal for a theme structure.

   There was little time. Cochran needed a proposal to present the next morning at a meeting of the management committee. Bebb and Denton set to work immediately after the meeting, one at either end of a conference table. Bebb, senior architect at Community Tectonics who counts among his credits exhibit design work for the 1933-34 Chicago Century of Progress exposition, drew rough sketches while Denton drafted a proposal describing what this structure could be. From the first glimmer of a concept, their ideas involved the sun. Since the Fair was to have an energy theme and the sun is the source of all energy, it seemed only natural to Bebb and Denton that the proposed structure represent and commemorate the sun. Bebb sketched a great golden sphere supported by a pedestal. Neither architect knew for sure at that point what the sphere would contain, but they knew already that they would call it the "Sunsphere". It was a good name, short and easy to say and remember. They wrote the name into the proposal, attached the sketch and dispatched a courier to slip them into the mailbox at Cochran's suburban Knoxville home within only hours of his request for ideas.

The next morning Cochran presented the Community Tectonics proposal to the other members of the management committee. They liked the idea immediately.

The committee knew that, historically, successful fairs had been centered on imaginative, beautiful "drawing cards" such as the Crystal Palace or the Eiffel Tower or, most recently, the Space Needle. They recognized in the Community tectonics proposal the beginnings of just such a central Fair attraction. The day after is inception, the Sunsphere project had a green light from the Fair's management committee, but, the long, difficult talk of turning the initial concept into reality had just begun.

Site selection was first on the agenda. High traffic flow was a major objective in placement of the Sunsphere on the 72 acre Fair grounds, which were at that point little more than a scraped out, meandering, mile-long valley separating downtown Knoxville from the nearby main campus of the University of Tennessee. Since the Sunsphere was to remain after the six-month fun of the fair as a centerpiece to the city park which was to be created from a central chunk of the Fairgrounds, consideration had to be given to easy accessibility for both visitors during the Fair and university students and Knoxvillians afterwards. The site chosen is the middle of the Fairgrounds, near other permanent Fair structures, new hotels, a convention center and parking garages, and is on a line between the campus and the busiest section of downtown Knoxville. The land chosen as the Sunsphere site was owned by several different owners. Untangling the legalities involved in buying the small but highly desirable parcel of land on which the Sunsphere was built was but the first of many complex problems the Sunsphere developers had to solve before construction could begin.

One such puzzle was financing. The Fair itself had set aside no money to build a theme structure like the Sunsphere. Community Tectonics was a healthy firm, but too small to bankroll such a big undertaking. Area banks had lent their limit to Fair-affiliated projects and, in any event, the entire project was as yet too speculative to inspire the confidence of investors. The best thing going for the Sunsphere in the spring of 1981 was a favorable feasibility study by a Washington consulting firm which said a well-planned tourist attraction such as the proposed Sunsphere could pay for itself if it included restaurants, observation decks and gift shops.

In the process of design research, the Sunsphere architects realized that the Sunsphere, when completed, would be the only multi-story, fully occupied spherical structure in the world. There have been many spherical and near spherical predecessors to the Sunsphere, some connected with past world's fairs. The vast buy nearly empty Perisphere of the 1939 New York World's Fair was temporary; the Atomium of the 1958 Brussels's World's Fair was a series of spheres. Buckminster Fuller's geodesic come pavilion at Expo '67 in Montreal, as innovative as it was, was only a partial sphere, or dome. And there have been spherical monuments, the last famous one a stainless steel openwork glove of the world, called the Unisphere, which was the symbol of the 1964-65 New York World's Fair. But never a permanent, single, multi-storied, habitable sphere. The revelation that the Sunsphere would be the first and only structure of its kind anywhere made the people at Community Tectonics determined to find a way to build it.

The problems of investors, financing, contractors, and design were wrestled with simultaneously. No investor cold sing on the dotted line without knowing that the project was workable and promising; no bank could lend money for construction without knowing exactly what the construction would cost and who would perform it; no construction company could commit to a construction cost figure without a detailed study of very precise blueprints and specifications; and those precise plans had to call for a design and building materials and construction techniques that added up to no more than what the budget allowed. All of these problems hinged on the biggest dilemma the Sunsphere architects faced—building codes.

No one at any time entertained any thought of building a structure that was any less than absolutely safe, but from the beginning the Sunsphere designers knew that they would have a difficult time meeting building code regulations. The reason was simple; the Southern Building Code was written to regulate conventional houses and office buildings and factories, not unusual structures like a golden glass sphere supported by towers. It was as if the Sunsphere architects were trying to bake a wedding cake according to a recipe for blueberry muffins; it could not be done. Or, at least, it seemed that the building codes were an insurmountable problem. The Community Tectonics architects met many times with city codes officials and committees. Outside consultants, such as a Nashville engineer who helped write both the National Fire Protection Association Code and the Southern Building Code, were hired to help. As every step the codes variance committees had to be convinced that the unique structure the developers proposed would meet the objectives, if not the letter, of the codes.

After months of hard work and setbacks, things began to look hopeful for the project. A final design was developed that satisfied codes officials, met budget restrictions and fulfilled the aspirations of the architects.

The architects had originally envisioned the Sunsphere as a golden glass sphere 86.5 feet in diameter, containing six interior levels and supported by a relatively low pedestal. This concept was modified several times during the process of design refinement. The most important change was the height of the Sunsphere. Building code regulations required that any building more than seven stories high had to be built of concrete, since concrete is fire-resistant. Unfortunately, the cost of a concrete pedestal for the Sunsphere was more than the construction budget allowed. The codes committee granted a variance to the Sunsphere architects only after they were able to convince the committee that they should consider only the number of stories in the sphere itself in their count. This permitted the architects to plan an open steel tower. It had also become apparent that if the Sunsphere was to achieve the landmark status its developers desired for it, it would have to be tall enough to rise above the other Fair buildings, many of which were to be remarkable structures themselves, and the planned high-rise convention center and hotel complex adjoining the Fair site. So the sphere rose to a height of 266 feet, almost 100 feet higher than originally planned. Elevating the globe of the Sunsphere made a smaller sphere more feasible; the planned diameter was reduced to 74 feet. The designers decided to abandon their plan to construct two of the levels of the sphere to revolve when they realized that the reduced diameter of the sphere alone, without revolving floors, would afford diners in any location on any level a spectacular 270-degree view of the Fair site, Knoxville and its suburbs and the hazy Smoky Mountains. Plans for a fast food restaurant at the base of the tower to serve Fair goers and park users were also added.

A group of local business people were approached as investors; they formed a partner-ship called Sunsphere, Incorporated, to back the project. First National Bank of Louisville, Kentucky agreed to lend the $5.2 million needed for development, construction and financing after the City of Knoxville agreed to lend the partnership $1 million of a federal grant, on a second mortgage, to help repay the Louisville loan. Stan Lindsey and Associates of Nashville were chosen as consulting structural engineers; West, Norris, Welch, and Miller of Knoxville were commissioned to serve as consulting electrical and mechanical engineers. Rentenbach engineering Company of Knoxville, the company responsible for managing construction for the entire Fair site, was contracted to construct the Sunsphere. In January of 1981, ground was broken on the site selected so many months earlier, and the Sunsphere began to rise out of the winter mud.

The 198-foot tower of the Sunsphere is hexagonal. From each point of the hexagon a steel column rises vertically to the base of the sphere. For the sake of speed and efficiency, the structural steel components of the tower were ordered in American Institute of Steel standard sizes. When the 600 tons of tower sections arrived in Knoxville, they were set in place and bolted together like a giant erector set. Two 418-step fire stairs and three glass-enclosed high-speed elevators are contained in the tower, which was painted blue in an effort to make it "disappear" against the sky; giving a floating effect to the sphere.

The patented framework system for the Sunsphere globe is based upon the most ancient post-and-beam construction techniques. Each floor within the sphere is supported by radiating beams cantilevered from the core of the sphere. The ends of these beams meet a series of evenly-spaced, curved tubular 'columns" that stretch from the sphere's "north pole" to its "south pole". The sphere is topped by a skullcap-like roof which covers heating and cooling equipment and elevator machinery. This skull cap section is painted the same gold color as the frames surrounding the panes of golden glass and is pierced at its top by a small well which conceals ventilation and exhaust outlets.

Real 14 karat gold gives the Sunsphere glass its rich, gorgeous color. The inner surface of each outer pane of glass on the sphere is lined with a vinyl film impregnated with gold dust. Because the glass is reflective, the apparent color of the Sunsphere varies from a brilliant metallic gold to a duller, paler gold, depending on the weather and time of day.

Finding gold-colored glass for the "skin" of the Sunsphere proved to be a much bigger problem than its designers anticipated. For months prior to the beginning of construction, Community Tectonics staffers searched for a manufacturer which could furnish golden glass to meet their specifications. They were told again and again that glass that would meet the highly specialized design requirements of the Sunsphere simply was not available. For one sad short period it seemed that the Sunsphere would have to be glazed with silver glass. Finally a New Jersey company was located to manufacture the nearly 14,000 square feet of reflective glass needed to enclose the sphere. Each pane of the beautiful glass cost, on the average, $1,000.

The Sunsphere glass system was developed especially for the project and is unique. Each unit of glass on the sphere consists of two quarter-inch panes of glass, one interior, one exterior, held in place by an aluminum frame, or mullion. On the top half of the sphere the outer-most pane of glass is tempered and the inside pane of glass is laminated. Between the two panes is an insulating airspace. Besides conserving energy, the design of the glass system also promotes safety. If, for example, a passing airplane lost a rivet which fell and hit the Sunsphere, diners inside would be safe. The exterior tempered glass on the upper half of the sphere would break into harmless small round pieces which would collect in the airspace and be prevented from falling into the restaurant itself by the laminated interior pane, which might crack after a blow but would remain intact. Since objects dropped from the interior of the sphere are the biggest threat to the glass in the lower half of the sphere, from the equator of the sphere down, the interior pane of glass is tempered and the outer pane is laminated.

Like the tower girders, both the glass panes and mullion sections were prefabricated by their manufacturers. The mullions have a baked-on finish in a shade of gold chosen to match the gold of the glass under as many different weather conditions as possible. The panes had to be cut to size before being either tempered or laminated. The 360 panes which enclose the Sunsphere were manufactured in seven shapes. One shape is a square-those panes run around the equator of the sphere. The other six shapes are trapezoids. To allow construction workers to install these various panes in their proper places, the glass manufacturer carefully numbered each pan according to its shape and what row above or below the equator it belonged. The last pane of the golden glass was installed in the sphere on February 19, 1982. All three local television stations sent news crews to cover the event. Knoxvillians had been watching the progress of the Sunsphere as carefully as Londoners watched the building of the Crystal Palace.

Considerable attention was given to making the Sunsphere energy efficient. Solar collectors were part of the original plans for the Sunsphere, but the cost of enough collectors to do the job in cloudy East Tennessee was prohibitive. The designers decided instead to concentrate on energy conservation. They were aided by natural attributes of the sphere. A sphere is the most heat0-conserving building shape because it presents the smallest possible surface area for the volume it encloses. Because it radiates much less heat from its surface, the Sunsphere retains more of the heat generated by its kitchens, occupants and lighting than would a rectangular structure of the same interior volume. The designers boosted the natural energy conservation capabilities of the sphere with their double-layer insulated glass system. The airspace between the panes retains interior heat, thus reducing the need for heat production during the winter. The gold outer pane reflects the heat-producing rays of the sun during the hottest parts of the year, reducing the need for air conditioning. Water source heat pumps furnish extra heat when it is needed. Water heated by the Sunsphere's air conditioning and kitchen equipment is circulated to heat the side of the sphere which is shaded. When the sun shades the other side, the process is reversed.

The Sunsphere was built to be extremely fire safe. A sprinkler system would extinguish most fires likely to occur, but several backup safety systems were included in the Sunsphere design. There is a smoke evacuation system to protect occupants from smoke inhalation. An interfloor speaker phone system allows for communication between firemen and occupants on other floors. Special drains were installed to catch water from the sprinkler system in order to prevent its freezing on the steel fire stairs in the event of a fire during cold weather. And every piece of elevator equipment is designed to function for a minimum of four hours during a fire—more than ample time to evacuate sphere occupants safely.

What you see in the Sunsphere depends on which of its elevators you board for a 43 second ride to the sphere interior.* One of the elevators goes to the bottom observation level, which is the first floor within the sphere and like a circular hallway. Visitors on this level are presented with a spectacular view of the Fair site and can even see the support tower beneath them through the sloping glass wall. During the run of the Fair, the Pennsylvania-based Sun Company, a broad-based multi-source energy company, sponsored energy education displays on this bottom observation deck, as well as on the top observation deck on the fifth floor of the globe and at the tower base near the elevators. *The elevators were changed in 1991.

Levels two, three and four of the sphere are reached by the dining room elevator. (these are also called levels five, six, and seven, if you count the three levels on the ground as the first three levels) The elegant Sunsphere Restaurant, which seats a total of 300 people, occupies the third and fourth levels. No on at any table on either level has a bad view. The panes of glass are so expansive at this point on the sphere that diners can see the beautiful view—on a good day, all the way to the Smoky Mountains, nearly 40 miles away—almost unimpeded by structural elements. Tables surrounding the sphere's core have been raised slightly to ensure that diners there have as good a view as those along the glass perimeter of each level. Since light passing through the gold glass seems to change many colors, the restaurant designers scrutinized every part of the restaurant décor, including carpeting and china and uniforms of restaurant personnel, under a sample of gold glass before making decorating decisions.

The kitchen for the restaurant is located on the second level. Hardee's the company which operates the Sunsphere restaurants under a 20-year lease, was forced to have some standard restaurant appliances modified or even specially constructed in order to fit the equipment they needed for a quality restaurant into the limited circular space. The VIP Lounge, an exclusive wedge-shaped, reservations-only dining room which seats only 40 people and has its own kitchen and serving personnel, is also on the second level. (also known as level 5, if you count the 3 levels on the ground)

The top level of the sphere, level five (or 8 if you count the 3 levels on the ground), is an observation level. It can be reached by the third of the Sunsphere elevators, which departs from the Clinch Avenue level entrance to the tower. All the elevators return to the arcade level where passengers walk across the pedestrian bridge. They can choose to go up one flight of stairs to Clinch Avenue or down one flight to the Hardee's fast food restaurant nestled in the base of the tower. This picturesque restaurant is like a sidewalk café beside the Fair's seven-acre Waters of the World Lake.

The Sunsphere is already a landmark. The curve of its golden sphere can be seen rising over the buildings surrounding it from almost any approach to the city. On sunny days it shimmers; at night it glows. And, *until someone builds another, it remains unique in the world, a modern spherical monument to the sun.

*Remember this was written in 1981. Another spherical tower was built in 2002 in Astana, Kazakhstan.

Jake Butcher in 2006 from the blog
BusinessTN Courtesy of Drew Ruble

In October 2011, photojournalist for the C Span Channel , Tiffany Rocque, interviewed Martha Rose Woodward about her research on the 1982 World's Fair for C Span Book TV. The program aired on 29th and November 1st nationwide.
Photo by Ashley Penery.

Barrett, age 13, and baby Erin--3 months old--my
children at the top of the Sunsphere. Ashley was
born in 1983.

MANY THANKS:

The following people were an integral part of this book, and for their help and input, I am forever grateful:

Barrett Buie, Erin Penery, and Ashley Penery: my three children who inspired me, took the journey along with me, and encouraged me to write this book.

Steve Hunley and Charmin Foth: Fountain City Focus

Bill Denton and Janice Sullivan of Denton &
Associates   Don Shell, Bill Vinson, Daryl Brady
Community Tectonics

Jesse Barr and Randy Tyree

Knoxville City Park Patrol: James Plankers

Public Building Authority, Jeff Galyon

Martha Rosson, Jenny Ball: East Tennessee History Center

Reference   Desk: Lawson-McGhee
Library   Phyllis   Garrison   (1935-2013)

Bill Cotter--photography

Sara Spangler--booking agent for the Sunsphere

Dan Andrews, photographer

Bibliography:

Alumnus Magazine, University of Tennessee,
1983. Ashe, Victor, e-mail interview, July 2007

Associated Press, "It's Original", 7-13-1984, Knox News-Sentinel, Knoxville, TN.

Aston-Wash, Barbara, "Art Meets Sky at Sunsphere," 5-8-1987, Knox News-Sentinel, Knoxville, TN. Barr, Jess, personal interview

Balloch, Jim, "Construction of convention center to close Sunsphere," 11-5-1999, Knox News-Sentinel, Knoxville, TN

Bayterek, google search

Beatley, Ernie, "Barr Engineered Expo Project Financing", 8-12-80, Knoxville News-Sentinel, Knoxville, TN

Brown, Fred, "Symbol of the City, 11-2002, Knox News-Sentinel, Knoxville, TN.

Childress, Mark, "Bringing the World to Knoxville," October 1981, Southern Living Magazine, Clinton Tribune, Morristown, Tennessee

Conley, Brian, "Reigniting the Sun," 7-13-2006, Metro Pulse,
Knoxville, TN Cystic Fibrosis Sponsor Sheet, Oct. 26,1986,
Knoxville, TN.

Daily Beacon, "Expo '82 Opponents Call for Referendum" 10-16-1978, University of Tennessee Student
Newspaper, Knoxville, TN

Dean, Jacquelyn, "Sunsphere Restaurant ,Lounge Are Proposed," 10-31-91, Knoxville News-Sentinel, Knoxville, TN

Dean, Jacquelyn, "2 Restaurants Compete for Sunsphere Space, 3-16-1994, Knoxville News-Sentinel, Knoxville, TN

Denton, William, architect, Morris & Associates, Morristown, Tennessee, personal interview, July 2007.

Durman, Louise, "Dining on High," 10-5-1982, Knox News-Sentinel, Knoxville, TN

Durman, Louise, "Best Eatin' Up and Down," 2-28-1982, Knox News-Sentinel, Knoxville, TN Efird, Paul, "Getting Around to Tough Task," 3-31-93, Knox News-Sentinel, Knoxville, TN Engineering News Record Magazine, 11-26-1981, McGraw-Hill, Anarbor, MI.

Fountain City Focus Newspaper, June, July, stories by Martha Rose Woodward

Harris, Roger, "Mortgage Owner Says Sunsphere Crunch at Hand", 1-15-85, Knoxville News-Sentinel, Knoxville, TN

Harris, Roger, "Owners "greedy", Mayor Sees Sunsphere Takeover," 1-6-1985, Knox News-Sentinel, Knoxville, TN.

Harris, R., "City Isn't Banking on Sunsphere Title," 8-20-86, Knoxville News-Sentinel, Knoxville, TN

Hetherington, Bob, "Sunsphere eatery closes with losses," 3-28, 1984, Knox News-Sentinel, Knoxville, TN

Higgins, Trevor, "Hootin', honkin' Sunsphere, Knoxville News-Sentinel, 12-30-03, Knoxville, TN. IBEW, "Skills of IBEW Members Helping Produce 1982 World's Fair, 7-81, Knoxville, TN. Johnson, Jennifer, "Sunsphere Climbers," 5-16-2000, Knox News-Sentinel, Knoxville, TN. Kauffman, Betsy, "Grandstanding on Baby Grand," 5-17-1990,

Knox News-Sentinel, Knoxville, TN. Kay, Paul, "Arts' Go Home to Sunsphere," Daily Beacon, 1-27-1987, Knoxville, TN.

Kenner, Randy, Press Release, 7-2007.

Knoxville Journal Knoxville, TN, Borrowed Time, Borrowed Money; the Fall of the House of Butcher, 1983.

Knoxville News-Sentinel, "Most of Those Polled…", 8-8-79, Knox News-Sentinel, Knoxville, TN. Lea, Sandra, Whirlwind, Butcher Banking Scandal, 2000

Lennox, Jeff, "Café and Catering," 5-10-2007, WATE-TV News, Knoxville, TN Maasrowe.com/EXPO.html, Bell MaaRowe Carillon, 5 10-2007.

Means, John, "Millions Granted For Expo 82," 10-4-1978, Knox News-Sentinel, Knoxville, TN

Park, Pam, "$1 Million Sunsphere Renovation on City Council's Agenda Tonight," 8-20-1991, Knox News- Sentinel, Knoxville, TN.

Park, Pam, "City Council Approves Lease of the Sunsphere," 8-21-1991, Knox News-Sentinel, Knoxville, TN

Patterson, Gene, WATE-TV News, personal interview, July 2007.

Reed, Vita, "Architect Will Study Sunsphere," 11-4-1990, Knox News-Sentinel, Knoxville, TN

Reed, Vita, "Visitors Center Preps for Move," 4-9-1992, Knox News-Sentinel, Knoxville, TN

Shell, Don, architect, Community Tectonics, Coward Rd. Knoxville, TN, personal interview, June 2007. Siler, Charles, "Hardee's Lease for Sunsphere Eateries Signed," 12-3-81, Knoxville News-Sentinel, Knoxville, TN

Siler, Charles, "Fair Site a Shadow of Its Former Self, 11-10-82, Knoxville News-Sentinel Knoxville, TN

Reese, M, "Knoxville's World's Fair, 1-1982, Newsweek Magazine

Trenda, Hilary, "Here We Go Again," Knoxville Voice Newspaper, 9-7-2006, Knoxville, TN. Tyree, Randy, personal interview, July 2007, Knoxville, TN.

Tyree, Randy, "World's Fair Was Appropriate Answer", 5-92, Knoxville News-Sentinel, Knoxville, TN Vaidya, Dipti, video tour, knoxnews.com/special/randomthis/d_sunsphere.shtml

Vines, Georgia, Sunsphere, 2-23-2000, Knox News-Sentinel, TN, Knoxville, TN WATE-TV web site

WIBR Web site

Williams, Tom, "City Agency Takes First Official Step Toward Foreclosure on Sunsphere," 1-19-1985, Knoxville News-Sentinel.

Williams, Tom, "Inspectors See Orange Over Sunsphere Sign," 10-21-1987, Knox News-Sentinel, Knoxville, TN.

Wilson, Lee, The Sunsphere and Other Structures, Morristown Printing Co., Morristown, TN, 1982. Wikipedia, org/wiki/Bayterek

Wikipedia.org/wiki/Kyle_Testerman

WIVK web site

Womack, Robert, "Sunsphere Expo Hub Approved," 11-16-1980, Knox News-Sentinel, Knoxville, TN Woodward, Martha Rose, Series of articles, Fountain City Focus Newspaper, June/July 2007, Knoxville, TN

www.tv.com/the-simpsons/bart-on-the-road/episode 1433

"Now he belongs to the ages"
(Statement made at the funeral of Abraham Lincoln)

As the mourners gathered around the coffin of Abraham Lincoln and laid him to his final rest, it is said that Secretary of War, Edwin Stanton said; "Now he belongs to the ages." Although the Sunsphere is not a national treasure, it is our treasure, and it does belong to us, the citizens of Knoxville, and to the ages that come after us.

Numerous people have asked me, why are you so interested in the Sunsphere? Or, why are you writing a book about the Sunsphere? The answer is easy, I am writing a book about the Sunsphere because I could not escape the overwhelming mental messages I kept getting, telling me to write a book about the
Sunsphere, write a book about the Sunsphere, write a book about the Sunsphere.

Once I set out on the path to write this book, I could not believe how events were put into my life, almost daily, that helped me. It was amazing to see that, just as I needed some information, or photos, or facts check, the things I needed would appear, as if out of nowhere. Truly, it was my destiny to write this book, and I am glad that I did.

As I come to the end of it, I send forward the story of the monument to the sun to current and future generations. After all, the youngsters who will be reading this book are also the very same people who will grow up one day and find themselves in leadership positions making decisions about the Sunsphere. They will also judge the decisions which were made by generations who have gone before them.

If the Sunsphere is anything, it is a length from the past that will stretch into the future. It is proof of what a group of people can do if they allow the creative, talented, intelligent individuals who live amongst them to flourish.

Regardless of who is in charge of the Sunsphere, it will continue to glisten in the sun, bringing beauty and mystery to those who live around it or who discover it for the first time.

To the Sunsphere, I say, "I have given you everything that I have got. I tried to "do you proud", as we say in the South. I salute you, my friend, and I love you. I know that you are listening, and I know that you love me too."

Retired Teacher Turns Writer

While wrestling with health issues retired school teacher Martha Rose Woodward turned her lifetime hobby of writing into a part-time career.

"It was on a fluke that I responded to a small ad for a part-time writer/reporter for a local, weekly newspaper," said Woodward.

"That decision has dramatically changed my life. I have found that I have an audience for my work. It is extremely rewarding to be able to express creative ideas while also getting paid."

While learning the new craft of journalism, Woodward soon developed a reputation as a skilled writer known for her depth of knowledge in historic research.

The hours she spent at the local libraries and the East Tennessee History Center helped her to publish two non-fiction books: Knoxville's Sunsphere in Sept. 2007 and Knoxville's 1982 World's Fair in Feb. 2009.

Her first novel, Even Wounded Birds Fly, debuted in April 2009.

"While doing work on the Sunsphere book I met many, very kind people who were willing to share details with me.

The publication of that book brought me my first professional contract as Arcadia Publishers from Mt. Pleasant, South Carolina had been searching for a writer to create a book about the 1982 World's Fair.

A friend of the editor told her about my Sunsphere book which he found on Amazon.com.

The editor contacted me and accepted my proposal. The 'Images of America' style book has done very well in sales," she said.

"People have fond memories of the 1982 World's Fair. It was an amazing event and is something our area can look back to with pride."Woodward currently works as a part-time freelance writer.

The Knoxville Journal Newspaper publishes three to four of her articles per week.

She has also sold stories to the Knox Focus Newspaper and the Seymour Herald Newspaper.

"I did not begin my career as a writer until two years ago at age 57," explained Woodward.

"Since that time, I have written and published 300 articles in newspapers, as well as writing five books—three of which have been published. My fourth book, a true crime story, will debut within the next month."

Woodward joined the Knoxville Writers' Guild in April of 2008 and was most recently voted as Education Committee Chairman.

"I am responsible for setting up workshops for Spring, Summer, and Fall," she explained.

"I recruit presenters, develop the schedules, and work with other members of the Guild to promote the events.

Part of the mission of the Guild is to promote the process of writing in the Knoxville area. We have meetings each First Thursday of the month.

Our yearly membership fee is $25 or $10 for students. I have had the wonderful opportunity to meet many talented and gifted writers and received help with my own needs."

Woodward can also be found on her blog at www.marthasunsphere.blogspot.com.

to editor@seymourherald.com

Martha Rose Woodward
939 Chickamauga Avenue
Knoxville, TN 37917

Photo taken by Bill Cotter.